DON'T LET MY BABY GO!

By

Yevette E. Fisher

DEVIL LET MY BABY GO!

Copyright ©2018
By Globe Shakers, LLC

This book or parts thereof may not be reproduced in any form, stored in a retrieval system, or transmitted in any form; electronic, mechanical, photocopy, recording, or otherwise is not permitted without prior written permission of the author.

Cover designed by Professional Identity Partners
Myprofessionalidentity.com

ISBN 978-0-9997545-0-4

©2018

All rights reserved

Printed in the United States of America

Names have been changed to protect the innocent

Table of Contents

Acknowledgments

First of all, I would like to give thanks to my Lord and Savior Jesus Christ. I give Him all the praise for keeping me through every test and trial. He is my rock, my strength, and my fortress. I put my trust solely in Jesus, and I never would have made it without the Holy Ghost.

To my late Mother, Lera Fisher, her support, prayers, and words of wisdom were priceless. She taught me that whatever I go through in life to always pray, and trust in the Lord. Mama would be very proud of what God has done in Nichol's life. Your memory is unfailing. I miss your smiling face. I will forever cherish our long conversations every morning as we shared our coffee and prayer over the phone. Rest in Heaven Mama.

Evangelist Ivy Allen, thank you for your wise council and countless prayers. You often took out time to talk with Nichol. Thank you for never being too busy to listen, and for every scripture that you spoke into my spirit to encourage me. You prayed with Nichol as a child to receive the Holy Ghost, so there was a special bond between you two. Thank you for the times you consoled me when I fell out on your office floor in despair. You often said, "We're not falling out 'til we have to." You kept me grounded by staying calm.

I thank the Lord for my friend Pastor Margie Jones, you were there when Nichol went out into the world. We worked together for thirteen years. You were one of my closest friends. You spent lots of time with her as a young girl when she was at the salon with us. I remember you did Nichol's hair for her senior prom. We worked side by side proclaiming the gospel to many, in spite of what was transpiring in my personal life. You were there through the pain and tears. Thank you for joining me in prayer and fasting on her behalf.

I want to thank my dear friend Sister Illona Hendrick, for always being a support in more ways than one. I appreciate your hospitality, kind words, and a good laugh over a cup of Starbucks coffee. Thank you for showing love to Nichol in spite of her choices. You constantly reminded her as she was growing up of your famous saying, 'In life there are choices, and with your choices, there are consequences.' No matter what she looked like, you and your family welcomed her into your home. Thank you for the many trips you and I took to get my mind off of my trials. I cannot thank you enough for the financial support over the years. You have been a friend that has gone above and beyond measure. God has sent you into my life as my guardian angel. You really know what it means to be a true sister in Christ. I thank the Lord for our friendship.

Thank you Sister Pamela Lishey, for the love shown towards Nichol and treating her as she was one of your own. I valued all the late-night conversations of encouragement. You and I must have witnessed to most of Los Angeles sharing 'The Good News' of Jesus Christ, be it in parks, beaches or around the kitchen table. We tag teamed well together. I thank God for all those early morning hikes and afternoon beach walks as we prayed about our problems. I am appreciative for all the many Thanksgiving and Christmas holidays you've shared with us. No matter Nichol's appearance, you constantly assured me that God was going to deliver her.

Evangelist Alice Shaw, thank you so much for your unfailing love towards Nichol and me. Your prayers and support were ordained of God. You had a way to bring calmness with prophetic music over a cup of hot tea. Your

4

door was always opened to be a help to whomever knocked. The memories we shared are unforgettable.

Evangelist Karolyn Chaney you have been a tremendous blessing to me down through the years. I want to give a heartfelt virtual hug and Thank You for your tireless dedication to this project.

Special thanks to Minister Rhonda Marie Quarles, Sister Mary Allen, Prophetess Lisa Van Dyke-Mitchell, Prophetess Menette Young, Evangelist Marvella Lipscomb, Sister Jennifer Griffin, Evangelist Wanda Lowery, and all the prayer warriors across the globe that continued to pray for Nichol's deliverance. God Bless Mother Pinkie Lee Geiggar, and thank you for your weekly phone calls and prayers. All those who dared to believe God on my daughter's behalf, I love and appreciate you!

A special thanks to my niece Tanesha Fisher Cager, who is like a daughter to me. Thank you for your constant concern for your cousin Nichol, and for being there whenever I needed a laugh, or smile. Also for all the gifts of love, every card, and the flowers you sent me on Mother's Day. You were a support to me on countless occasions through many family tragedies. May God's blessings overtake you!

Foreword

Evangelist Waters is a strong prophetic intercessor. This book will give any person hope. Twenty years is a long time to believe God to manifest a miracle. She stood the test of time! I cried as I read this book. I am the daughter she is writing about. As her "only" child, I never realized the anguish she experienced. My own selfish desires took my Mom through hell and back.

Mom is a real trooper. She never gave up on me, seizing the opportunity to lay hands on me with anointing oil every chance she got. I cannot repay the Lord for what He has done, but I owe him Praise! God couldn't have given me a better Mother to endure the warfare that was assigned to take me out.

This book is emotional and transparent. This woman of God's constant opposition with demonic forces was intense. Every child should read this to feel the heartbeat of a parent. Every parent will gain strength, wisdom, and tools to combat the snares of the enemy.

"Her children arise up, and call her blessed."
Proverbs 31:28

J. Nichol Collins
Author of Behind Enemy Lines

Introduction

My purpose for writing this book is to be a support system to all those parents that may feel alone. I want to share how I was affected by my daughter's decision to live a homosexual lifestyle. She lived in perversion for twenty years. I am often asked the question, 'How did you do it?' or 'What was your reaction when you found out that your daughter was gay?' I wish my response was that I was a calm and confident parent; or that I could say, 'It was just a piece of cake.' I dare not lie and tell you I always trusted the Lord.

However, that would be so far from the truth. The words that come directly to mind are shock, devastation, disappointment, and heartbroken. Oh, and let us not leave out the word "embarrassed." It felt like her decision was a reflection on me as a parent. Somehow, I felt I had failed.

Our pastor lived and taught a life pertaining to Holiness. He preached against "all" sin, including what the Bible taught about homosexuality. I believed Nichol was knowledgeable that living a gay lifestyle was a sin. The last thing I expected was for her to get involved in such an abominable transgression. Nonetheless, that bold spirit stared me in my face.

It all happened so quick. The hardest thing to accept, was that it unfolded right under my nose. My daughter was with me most of the time. We were very close. Nichol is my only child, so we practically did everything together. When I moved, she basically was one step behind me.

The enemy is such a 'liar and deceiver.' He does not care who he attacks. The Devil is going around seeking whom he may devour. He patiently waits for a crack to squeeze through to tear up our lives. He tries to catch us off guard. If he can't get to those of us that are strong, then he makes plans to attack whoever is dear to our heart. His attack may include: our marriages, children, finances, and health.

My desire in recounting the events in my life is that someone might be encouraged to learn how you can be victorious through whatever test you may encounter. God is a mighty deliverer! He can do exceedingly, abundantly, more than we can ask or think. He will never put more on us than we can bear. Trust me, I know that when the fire is turned up to the tenth degree, and it seems all those scriptures are irrelevant, I have found the word of God to be true. As I share my story, I pray that someone will be inspired to intercede for their child, and not give up on them.

Meeting Skipper Dipper

I remember as though it was yesterday. It was the summer of 1969 when the Fisher family moved into town. My parents had eleven children, all one year apart from each other. I was the third oldest, with eight brothers and two sisters. Our family moved from Long Beach, California, which was a diverse community to Compton. It was a culture shock for us to move to a city that was predominantly black. The house only had three bedrooms and one bathroom. My father told the landlord he only had a few children. It was hard to find someone to rent to such a large family.

There was a guy that lived in my neighborhood, I had been watching. There was a clear view of his house from my front door. One afternoon, I was outside on my porch and I noticed this "fine dude" (as we called boys in those days). He was walking up the street wearing dress clothes, which was unusual.

As a teenager no one else in the neighborhood dressed like him. He was so neat. He had on a nice black leather trench coat. I considered that to be apparel you might wear for a special occasion. He certainly caught my attention. As he walked past we made eye contact. I would smile, but he never stopped. I watched him walk past my house a few more days.

I noticed him again walking past my house. This particular day, I decided to approach him. One of my younger brothers was riding his bike outside.
"Give me your bike I need to use it," I said.

I wanted to follow the young man to the store. I was curious to know his name. He had on a blue dress shirt with his sleeves rolled up, blue dress slacks, and nice polished black dress shoes. Afros were in style at the time, and his Afro was cold-blooded. He was so neat and clean. I had never seen a boy dressed like that in the middle of the week.

On the other hand, I dressed like a typical thirteen year old. I had on a pair of cutoff jeans rolled up to my thigh, a tank top, knee-high socks, and casual shoes. It was proper attire in the summertime. I rode the bicycle up the street to the store, which was just a few houses away. I finally caught up with him.

"Hello, what's your name?" I asked.

"What's up? My name is Skipper Dipper the honey-dripper," he replied, in a cool smooth tone.

I began to strike up a conversation with him. I was just a foolish thirteen year old, flirting with a fifteen year old boy. I finally met my mysterious crush. Little did I know, this would be the beginning of a childhood love affair that would change my life forever.

Skip and I began spending more time together that summer. There were different street boundaries that determined what school you attended. One main street separated us. I was in junior high school which went up to the 9th grade. In those days, high school started at the 10th grade. The following year, Skip and I were high school sweethearts. I was a sophomore, and Skip was already a senior.

Skip was ahead of his time. He was extremely mature for his age. He hardly ever went to class, and hung out at the back gate of the school where the big yellow buses dropped off the students and all the action took place. Guys in "low-rider" cars pulled up to drop off their under aged girlfriends. The cars played loud music on their eight tracks. All you heard was "Hey Love," by the Delfonics.

Skip never wore blue jeans, and always had on dress slacks. He sometimes wore a black brim hat, and nice waist line leather jacket. I discovered later, that he was selling pills called "red devils." By the time I entered high school it was official that I was "Skip's lady."

Over a period of time, he became possessive and controlling. He was very jealous, insecure, and allowed his temper to get the best of him. Our relationship escalated early on from verbal to physical abuse. The summer that we met, I had lost my virginity to Skip at the age of thirteen. Of course, in his mind, I belonged to him. We were not grown-up enough to handle being in a serious relationship. We were just two children playing dress-up at school.

There were days that we got into arguments at school. When I got off the school bus, Skip would already be there with his Doberman Pinscher named Nomad. He would chase me home like a mannish little boy. The abuse escalated as time went by.

After my high school graduation our tumultuous relationship continued. We eventually decided to move in together, despite the abuse. We fought, broke up, and dated other people. It was an unhealthy "soul tie." I cannot explain it, we were not good together. It was toxic. Yet, we somehow, ended up back together after every episode.

Skip professed to be a Black Muslim, though he did not practice their teachings. I eventually realized he was all messed up in the head. He did not want to get married because he said that was the "white man's rules."

"We are married in our hearts Yevette," Skip said.

"You're right Skip," I replied.

I was brainwashed by him. He manipulated me into believing whatever he said was the gospel truth.

Marriage was not something I wanted to do anyway. I believe my perception of marriage was altered due to being the oldest girl of 10 siblings. Growing up I practically ran the household because my parents both worked long hours. Most girls had a dream of the white picket fence, a few kids running around the house, and a dog. That was not my dream at all.

I saw a bad example of married life from my mother

11

and father. My father was verbally abusive, and insanely jealous over my mother. They constantly argued. At times, it was so bad Mama would pack us up and leave my father. My father would find us, they would make up, and another baby was born. That cycle went on until they ended up with eleven children. I always said at an early age that I never wanted to get married or have kids.

My Parents Price & Lera Fisher

I graduated Class of 1973 Compton High School

Edward Lee Collins AKA "Skip"   Yevette Fisher (Me)

Beautiful Arrived

When Skip and I graduated we moved in together. When Skip decided it was time for us to have a baby, he talked me into getting off birth control. I got pregnant right away. He put many demands on me as to how his child would to be raised. He also made me promise that I would take care of "his" baby if anything should ever happen to him. He acted like he had some weird premonition that he would not be around to raise a child.

A few days prior to giving birth, I was in a car accident. We were hit from behind. The Devil tried to kill my baby before she got here. I refused medical attention at the scene of the accident. Hours later, I went into labor. My baby was knocked out of the birthing position, which caused complications in my delivery. After twenty-two hours in labor, the decision was made that I would have a cesarean-section. We named her Jamila Nichol Collins. She looked like a little Indian baby. Jamila meant "Beautiful" in Arabic. Her Dad named her after the famous boxer Muhammad Ali's daughter.

In our circle of friends, it was a big deal for the child of Skip and Yevette to be born. We were a popular couple, and our peers were excited to see her. When the nurse showed Jamila Nichol to me she looked as though she had been on this planet before. Her expression, if it were to be read, said, 'What are y'all looking at?' She wasn't wrinkled up, nor did she have that spacey, clueless look that newborns have. There was something different about this baby. I remembered saying, "Ohhh…she's so beautiful," just before passing out from the medication.

Two Peas in a Pod

Nichol and I were bonded from the womb. There was something about being a mother that instantly changed my life. I never knew that having a child could be so fulfilling. My way of thinking shifted once I became a parent. Skip was no longer the top priority in my life.

I had this little helpless child that was depending on me to protect and care for her. I realized that the decisions I made affected the future of my child. When I met Skip, I was just a thirteen year old kid. Before I knew it, I was the mother of an infant daughter. Nine years of my life had passed by.

I wasted a lot of years going in circles with an intelligent man who had no ambition. He clearly was not an upright citizen. My focus turned toward Nichol, and my view on life became very serious overnight. I asked myself, 'Do you want to raise your daughter in an environment surrounded by drugs and abuse?' A lot of dynamics came with the drug lifestyle: parties, late phone calls from customers, and the constant entertaining of friends.

Shortly after Jamila Nichol's birth, Skip started to experiment with a new drug called PCP (embalming fluid). He always sold drugs, but usually it was marijuana. Don't get me wrong, marijuana was not legal in the 70's, but he took it to another level with PCP. He began to sell it, and use it. Skip's behavior became very erratic.

I recall going out to a club one night. Skip never liked to dance. Suddenly, he broke out dancing, took his shirt off on the dance floor, and swung it around in the air. He was discombobulated and delusional. He had no idea where he was or who he was. When we made Skip put his shirt on it was backwards. I knew then that PCP was not just a recreational drug. His behavior was strange, especially for a guy that did not dance. In the 70's, we as "black folks" did not get that wild on the dance floor.

Skip's behavior became progressively worse. I had endured years of abuse, black eyes, beatings with belts, and being backhanded for no reason. On many occasions, I was left with a bloody nose. I once was chased out the house practically naked to escape from Skip's angry rant. It was unbearable. I knew if I did not get out now, me or my baby could possibly end up dead. Finally, I made the decision to leave him. The number one priority in my life was Nichol.

Nichol was less than a month old, we had company over. Skip was high off the drug PCP. He entered the living room in his underwear.

"I am Jesus, look it's a star in my underwear," Skip said, looking spaced out.

"Oh, okay, well go back in the room and get dressed honey," I said.

He continued to babble on with foolish talk. There was a fear that came over me. I knew now for sure it was time to go. That incident was the straw that broke the camel's back. Our childhood relationship had run its course. I packed up my baby's things, and left with only our clothes. I drove to my mother's house.

Little Character

Nichol was a very advanced child. At seven months old she was walking around the house, had a full set of teeth, and was aware of what was going on around her. I enjoyed watching her grow so rapidly. Nichol was a happy baby, and she laughed all the time. I cherished being her mother.

I remember celebrating her 1st birthday party at Mama's house. It was a small gathering with my family. I bought a cake from the bakery, and placed a big #1 wax candle on it. I got Nichol all dolled up in a beautiful dress. I put the cake in front of her, and allowed her to gouge into it with her hands. She had icing all over her face. I took pictures on my Kodak camera with the cube bulb on top.

My mother was furious. She thought it was such a waste of cake and money. However, I was determined to spoil, love, and raise Nichol like I wanted to. I gave her a birthday party every year. I wanted my baby to have all the things that I lacked coming up.

When Nichol began to talk, it was as though she just opened her mouth and started speaking clearly. It was never baby talk. She had a memory like an elephant. If you did not want something repeated, you better not say it in front of Nichol. She would say it verbatim. I used to buy children's books to read to her at night before she went to bed. She memorized the entire story.

I recall taking her to doctor appointments, and she was reading her book in the waiting room. People were astonished at how well this two year old could read. They had no idea that they were being bamboozled. It was quite comical watching her so animatedly reciting stories as she stared at the pages.

My mama recognized that Nichol was advanced

beyond her years. She suggested I take her to be tested at the UCLA medical center, but I refused. I did not want to make her into some sort of science project. Her Grandma Wyatt on her father's side would often tell me how brilliant the members in Nichol's family were. They had very high IQ's. "They're geniuses," she would say. I was young, so I thought maybe she was just bragging on her grand baby. As time passed, it was apparent that Nichol was a child prodigy.

My Brother Dwight

My 1st Love Skip & Our Baby

Amtrak & Jack

Eventually one of my older cousins help me land a job at Amtrak National Railroad Passenger Corporation. This job afforded me the means to get my own place for my daughter and myself. Skip was obsessed with me, and was determined not to let me go that easily. He made it very difficult to cut ties completely.

I started working at Amtrak Reservation & Information Bureau. They trained groups of new hires in a classroom setting. The same day I started a man named Jack Rivers was hired. For the next three months we completed a training course before going out on the floor to man the phone lines.

There were about fifteen of us in the class hired at the same time. Jack made it clear the very first week of training that he was interested in me. He did not say anything directly to me right away. Jack had a subtle way of flirting; like the way he passed an ink pen to me, or how he looked when I asked him a question. His attraction to me was obvious.

When we hired in, Jack dressed appropriately to get through probation. He wore nice suits, checkered shirts, and his hair was in a neat Afro. After we passed the probation period Jack busted up in the office in an orange jumpsuit. It was zipped halfway down his chest, his hair that used to be neatly packed down, was blown out like a wild man. Somehow, that little incident sparked my curiosity about this "Jack Rivers." Funny how some girls like a "bad boy."

Jack made several advances towards me throughout the three months we were in the class. Once we passed our probation period he pursued me even harder. Jack was a very handsome man, but he was not my type. He had a light complexion with beautiful curly hair. I preferred a chocolate

21

guy. The women in the office of all nationalities flirted with him, even some of the gay men were attracted to Jack.

One day, I was in the break room using the pay phone. Jack was taking a nap with a newspaper over his face. He overheard me pleading with Skip to return my car that he had taken when I stopped at a red light on my way to work. Before the day was over Jack approached me.

"Are you alright? Do you need any help? Jack asked, concerned.

"No thank you, but thanks for asking," I replied.

I thought to myself, 'he's such a nice guy, so helpful.'

Jack always wanted to help people. It had got around the office that he prepared income taxes. Several coworkers often asked for help with their taxes. Jack helped people without charging for the information.

As time went by Jack continued to flirt with me. He was very persistent. Outside of work I did some modeling jobs on occasion. I was young, thin, and cute. As a twenty-two year old single mother, I enjoyed the attention from Jack. I was being a tease, but that is as far as I had planned to take it.

I was not attracted to Jack, and besides he was married. Jack had three children by two different wives. He had two sons while in high school and the boys were only two weeks apart. He married both their mothers at some point. He later had a daughter with his second wife whom he was married to when I met him.

Every Thursday, I went to my job to pick up my paycheck. My brother's girlfriend Diane rode with me one week to get my check. She met Jack, and he had on checkered pants with a "pleather" coat. Jack followed me down the elevator to my car. He certainly had a way with the ladies, my little sister was smitten with his smile, deep sexy voice, and demeanor.

"Girl he sure is fine," Diane said.

"He's alright, but not my type," I said.

"You should go out with him, he is nice," Diane said.

"Girl, he's married, and I'm not interested in him anyway," I said.

Dating a married man never was my thing. Besides, I had several men interested in me. I never needed to take someone else's husband. My options were plentiful in that era.

A few weeks later my little sister Diane passed away suddenly. She was at a friend's house taking a nap. A blood clot traveled to her heart and killed her in her sleep. My family was devastated. Diane was like family to us. She and my younger brother Ross had dated since their early teens. They had a three year old daughter together.

Diane's death deeply affected me. In my grieving state and twisted thinking, I somehow wanted to honor her last request before she died. I convinced myself that Diane was "young" ...only twenty. At the time, I was about twenty-three. The thought came to me, 'Who's to say I won't die young?' 'Diane said, I should just go on one date with Jack, since he's not happy at home anyway.' How crazy is that?

After Diane's funeral I returned to work. Jack was determined to win me over. He shared his homemade lunches with me almost every day. I believe I was a challenge for him because he was not use to being rejected by women.

After living at Mama's house a few months, I was ready to move. My daughter and I needed our own space. Skip's sister, Joyce and I were still very close. We used to hang out together when we were teens. We graduated from high school the same year. She was married, and her husband owned some duplexes. They agreed to rent one to me and Nichol. At the time it did not cross my mind that there would be a problem because she was Skip's sister. Their family was aware of his abuse and supported me wholeheartedly.

The Hook Up

Jack continued flirting with me at work. The subject came up if I could cook. Jack hinted around that he wanted me to cook for him in the near future. Remembering that I promised Diane I was going to give Jack a chance, I went against my better judgment. I invited him over for dinner. He did not hesitate to take me up on that offer.

I believe it was on a Friday night, Jack showed up not a second late. I told him to have a seat, and make himself at home. I went to the kitchen to check on the food. When I came back to the living room, Jack was standing up stark, butt naked! It was like a scene in a movie. From that very day, Jack never left my house.

I remember the popular movie "Harlem Nights." There was a woman named Sunshine that had sex with a Caucasian guy. Afterwards, the guy called his house and said to his children, 'Put your mother on the phone.' When his wife came to the phone he told her, 'I'm never coming home again, I will be by to pick up my things.' Jack literally did the same thing! A few days later, I allowed Jack to move in lock, stock, and barrel.

I was afraid of my abusive ex-boyfriend Skip. He just would not leave me alone. He became a stalker in the worse sense. I figured if I had a man living with me Skip would not bother me anymore.

As time went by, Jack grew on me. I fell head over heels in love with him and believed I had found my soul mate. We did everything together. The relationship took me by storm. I lived and breathed Jack Rivers. We worked together, partied together, spent our weekends at parks and beaches. We had romantic dinners at some of the finest restaurants in Los Angeles. He was such a romantic guy.

"You don't have to get a babysitter, bring the baby with us," Jack said.

That was one of the things that drew me even closer to him. Not only was he interested in me, but he wanted to be a dad to my child. Being with Jack was like taking a roller coaster ride. Eventually, that ride later turned into "The Colossus" ...up and down, in and out, round and around we went. Never a dull moment.

Suburbs

Jack and I moved out of Joyce's duplex to the suburbs. As Nichol became old enough to go to school we had relocated to Orange County. The children were predominantly Caucasian, and the parents were affluent. Moving to that area gave Nichol the opportunity to be exposed to a better education. She received a good scholastic foundation. Since she was a fast learner, she read and spelled quite well. Nichol was articulate with an outstanding pronunciation. It was clear that she was not like most children her age.

Jack's dad offered to rent us the house that Jack was raised in. We later decided to move to Pasadena, California which is known as "The City of Roses." This is where the Rose Bowl Parade, and football games would be held every year on New Year's Day. Nichol was privileged once again to attend some of the better public schools available at that time. Linda Vista Elementary was overlooking the Rose Bowl.

My mother liked Jack, but she advised me not to take my young daughter out to the suburbs; with a man that had teenage boys, and a bunch of dogs. I was in love, convincing myself it would work. Away to the "City of Roses" I went.

Pasadena was a nice place to raise children. The only complaint I had was that all of Jack's family lived there. Jack's ex-wife that he abandoned lived about five minutes from us. Jack's father was close by, and his mother was a lesbian with a live-in "girlfriend."

I was so young and naive. I did not realize what I was getting myself into. I moved right into the enemy's camp. Jack seemed to operate two households. He was not legally divorced yet, so whenever the wife called he went running.

It was his world. All his friends lived there, and his family business was there.

I grew weary of all the drama, and gave Jack an ultimatum. "Either we get married or let me go." Jack made the decision to get a divorce. He did not want to lose me. We lived together about five years toiling back and forth with the decision to marry or not. Jack had already been married twice. I would be wife number three, so he was hesitant.

I never was one that had childhood dreams of marriage, but I was in love. I assumed that since I had a daughter to raise, this would be the best thing to do. Though we loved each other, we should have let it go long before we did. The relationship had way too many dynamics for a healthy union. The chemistry between us was too strong to break away. Jack was being selfish. He wanted his cake and to eat it too. I did not consider the consequences that would result in a blended family.

After many tears, and restless nights, Jack finally popped the question. Of course, my answer was 'yes.' We had a big church wedding, and held our reception in our back yard. Jack's three children and Nichol were in the wedding. I had six bridesmaids. Nichol and her step-sister were the flower girls. On a beautiful hot day in June, Jack and I were married.

Impacted

I was more like a friend, but still a parent to Nichol. She shared everything with me. I would play with her, and her toys for entertainment. We spent time at the park often having picnics. Many nights we had slumber parties in her room as we ate homemade cookies that Jack made. She did not require many spankings. She was an obedient child. Nichol did not give us any trouble, she did her homework, and chores without being told.

Jamila Nichol was six years old, when Skip was killed in a drug related incident. His neighbor two doors from his mother's house shot him in the head. He was twenty-nine years old. It was Easter weekend when they had Skip's funeral. Although, I had moved on with my life, it was devastating to hear about his death. After all, I spent all my teen years with him.

Jack was very supportive of me and Nichol when Skip died. I was still very close to Skip's family. His mother was like another mother to me. Nichol was sad. She was too young to really understand, but of course, I was there to support her. His family suggested I ride in the family car with Nichol. The last ride that we took was through our neighborhood where we met when I was thirteen. We even passed by the high school we had attended. The memories were bittersweet. I had always hoped that Skip would turn his life around.

The month prior to Skip's murder, I lost my father to cancer. Skip was at my father's funeral service. Nichol ran and jumped into his arms. For some reason it seemed as though she was never going to see her father again. My mother even made a statement I thought was strange at the time.

"Ummm, Nichol ran to her father as though she ain't gonna ever see him again," Mama said, chuckling.

There was a bit of humor to what my Mother said at the time. However, those words stayed with me. Losing our fathers, a month apart drew Nichol and me even closer. Very rarely did you see one of us and not the other. Wherever I went, Nichol came right along with me. I loved my child.

By the time Nichol was seven years old my life changed drastically. I wanted to lose ten pounds, and was led by the Lord to a weight loss clinic. The owner, named Sister Dale was a prophetess. She shared the fullness of the gospel with me. She invited me to meet her at an Apostolic-Holiness church on a Monday night for a prayer service. After work, I went directly to the church.

I was born again. I had been baptized in the name of Jesus a few years prior at another Apostolic church. I completed my salvation by being filled with the Holy Ghost. Acts 2:38 says, "Repent and be baptized every one of you in the name of Jesus Christ for the remission of sins, and you shall receive the gift of the Holy Ghost."

I came home a changed person. It seemed that my life was transformed overnight. I never went back to the way I was living. No more sin for me. I was so excited. I finally found that peace that I was searching for. I will never forget how I felt on the drive home. I spoke in tongues all the way to my house on the freeway. I walked into the house. Fell on the bed next to my husband Jack.

"I got saved," I said, with great relief.

"That's nice honey. Now come to bed," Jack said, as he patted me on my head.

I'm sure Jack was thinking 'saved, again?'

I was already a member at a Baptist church, and now I was telling him I got saved. Ever since he had known me, it seemed like I got "saved" every six months. I always had a form of Godliness. I was raised up in church. My Grandfather was a Methodist Pastor, and he baptized all the grandchildren by sprinkling them over a gold basin. I knew in my heart this time there was a difference. I felt totally complete.

My life never was the same again.

I left my Baptist church, and became a member of the Apostolic church where I received the Holy Ghost. My husband Jack did not join right away, he was always a bit of a skeptic when it came to religion. My lifestyle change caused major problems in my marriage. I no longer indulged in the same things Jack and I were accustomed to enjoying together. Things got bad between us.

Nichol began to love our new church. Within three months, she was compelled to be baptized in the name of Jesus. She begged me every Sunday to let her get baptized.

"Mommy please let me get baptized," she pleaded.

"No, you are too young Nichol," I said.

I finally gave in. Nichol and two of my brothers were baptized the same day. Seven months later she was filled with the Holy Ghost; with the evidence of speaking with other tongues. We both were on fire for the things of God. Nichol began to share the Gospel with her cousins, and peers at school. Many people were saved because of us sharing the good news of Jesus Christ's death, burial, and resurrection.

We took neighbors, and friends to our church. Our car was filled just about every Sunday with young people, most of whom got saved. It was so gratifying to see God's hand move and draw people to the kingdom. Nichol and I were on a mission.

A friend of mine at our church had a dream about Nichol.

"Yevette, is your daughter's last name Collins?" she asked.

"Yes," I replied.

Her eyes got big.

"Wow!" (She started speaking in tongues.) "Girl, I dreamed I was in heaven and I saw the name 'Jamila Collins' in the clouds written in the twelve foundations with the Apostle's," she said.

"What? Really that's interesting," I said.

I realized it was something special about my daughter pertaining to a work for the Lord. That was not ordinary for someone to dream of a name that they did not know. Jamila Nichol Collins, from the foundation of the world was chosen by God. I was such a new convert I did not know how to guard the peculiar anointing on her life.

Our Pastor's wife started a program called "Big Sister, Little Sister." The first lady picked Nichol. This was a program where each woman chose a girl under the age of eighteen and mentored her. Nichol started to spend lots of time with the first lady and her daughters. Over time, Nichol became a family favorite. She spent a lot of time with the Pastor's family, including some holidays.

I was praying with Sister Dale one day at her weight loss clinic. She had a vision.

"I see a woman with wavy black hair, clear eyes and smooth brown skin. Do you know anyone that looks like that?" she asked.

"Hmmm, sounds like Joan my husband's ex-wife," I replied.

"No, this is an older lady that will be spiritually instrumental and sent by God into your life," she said.

"Oh, okay amen," I said.

"When you meet her, you will know it's her," she said.

Shortly after receiving that prophecy, I went to pay my car note. The bank teller would not process my payment without the coupon book. I was frustrated trying to get to work. She insisted that this was needed to make a payment. God's divine timing orchestrated all of this.

I had to go all the way back home to get the booklet. When I pulled into my driveway, this woman was talking to my husband in the front yard. He was pulling fruit off the trees to give her. She started prophesying to him about things in his life, he quickly avoided any further conversation.

"You should be talking to my wife," Jack said, chuckling as

he backed away from her.

At that moment my eyes connected with the woman. I knew this was the lady Sister Dale had seen in the vision. We instantly connected that day. She introduced herself as Mother Sims. I discovered she lived on my street for years, but I never saw her until that day. I felt a heavy Godly presence as she spoke.

Weeks later I saw Mother Sims out working in her garden. I pulled to the curbside to say hello. She came over to the car, and glanced at my daughter Nichol in the backseat. "The Devil is going to try and kill this child! You need to go on a fast for this baby not for anything else but her. Don't pray for your husband or nothing else; this fast is strictly for your daughter. Obey the prophet, and so shall you prosper. Now go on, I'll talk to you later" she said, adamantly.

"Oh, okay yes ma'am," I replied, puzzled.

I pulled off thinking, 'I wonder what this is all about because my daughter is sweetly saved."

I did go on that fast because I realized she was a true woman of God.

Wedding Day w/Jack

Nichol & Grandma Wyatt
@Church Coronation Ball (Skips mom)

Skip is Gone but not Forgotten

My Dad Price Fisher Forever in my heart   All 8 of my Brothers 2 sisters at the Funeral

Teen Years

Nichol had boyfriends growing up in church, and some from school. Sometimes a boy would come by the house. My husband and I allowed them to play video games in her room. I dropped her off to spend time with one guy when his parents were home. She was attracted to boys, but I cannot say she was ever in love as a teenager. When we went to various conventions, she met other young men from various states.

Nichol was a typical teenager, talking on the phone for hours to boys. I made the mistake of giving her a phone line once, because she had a good report card. She hardly ever came out of her room. Having her own phone did not last long. Nichol's grades dropped in one semester. I disconnected that phone line.

One year I went to a women's retreat. Sister Dale and I shared a room together. While we were eating breakfast with everyone in the dining hall she leaned over to relay a word from the Lord to me.

"The Lord said Jack and Nichol will be your greatest opposition as you walk with God. I don't know any details, but stay strengthened in prayer," she said.

I remembered what Mother Sims told me, and became a little fearful of the future. I saw no signs at the time of what might be getting ready to transpire.

I kept a pretty good tab on Nichol. I knew her whereabouts most of the time. She played on the girls' basketball team in high school. She had one close friend that she hung around with named Shelly that lived two blocks away.

Nichol was different and tried to fit in at school.

"Mom, everyone on the team says a curse word when we're

playing basketball. Can I just use a few curse words Mom? Please?" Nichol pleaded.

"No, girl, you can't do that, you're saved." I said.

"The coach curses, so why can't I use a word or two?" she asked.

"You are different Nichol stop trying to follow the crowd," I said.

"Well how about ditching school? Some of my friends invited me to a 'ditch day' for pizza, but I told them I would ask my mom," she said.

"You cannot miss school girl," I laughed.

She was so clueless and transparent with me. Days later she was glad she was not at the ditch day.

"Mom do you know they had boys over there? she said, shocked.

"Well, yeah that's what they do at these gatherings Nichol that's why I didn't want you there," I said.

The kids teased Nichol for being different. Her friends knew she went to church. They called her "church girl."

When Nichol was in middle school we started going to a service in Palm Springs, California. That service was geared around the youth; however, all ages attended the service. People came from California, Nevada, and Hawaii. We loved going to Palm Springs. It became a yearly trip for us for the next eight years. She had a ball.

I tried not to be too strict on Nichol. I allowed her to attend school dances, and sporting events. She also loved hanging out downtown at the movies with her friends. Pasadena was a small city, so we easily dropped her off and picked her up in no time.

As Nichol grew in the things of God she became very involved in our church. Nichol attended Sunday School weekly. We both went to church for morning and evening service. She joined the choir, but could not hold a note. Instead, the junior usher board became more her speed. She was active in various youth activities. She was asked to speak at a Youth Christmas Dinner one year.

In her early teens it was revealed to Nichol that she was called to ministry. She attended an adult bible college in high school. Her future was looking bright. People young and old constantly complimented me on what a nice girl Nichol was. Nichol and I had a good mother-daughter relationship. Often, other mothers asked me for advice about how to develop a closer relationship with their daughters. I felt blessed to be her mother.

Nichol's whole life revolved around church. In the Summer, she attended vacation bible school. At the end of the summer, the church rewarded the kids with various trips to: Magic Mountain, Knott's Berry Farm, and Raging Waters. We attended church picnics, weddings, bridal showers, gospel concerts and whatever else was on the calendar, we were there.

Nichol had her driver's license at sixteen. Whenever I could not attend something at church she was able to drive herself. I never had to worry about where she was. Nichol could frequently be found somewhere around the church. She did not mind helping at weddings, bridal showers, or whatever else they needed.

On Saturday's Nichol came to work with me at the Salon. We had lots of fun with customer's and employee's. It was in the heart of South Central Los Angeles. On the same lot, World on Wheels Skating Rink was next door. Nichol sometimes made extra money from the other stylist by sweeping up hair after a haircut or going to get lunch for them. My co-workers loved her at the shop she kept us in stitches. Never a dull moment at Trina's Beauty Salon.

8th Grade Graduation   9th Grade Dance

Divorce

By the time Nichol was in the tenth grade Jack and I had run our course. We decided to throw in the towel after fifteen years together. We got divorced and Nichol and I moved to Los Angeles. Our church was in Los Angeles, as was my job, and most of the people I associated with.

The Lord blessed us to move to a nice area. The rent was very expensive, but it was worth every dollar. The apartment was the size of a house. It had two large bedrooms and two full baths. There was a security door, where a person had to buzz into the apartment. We also had a sauna, and underground parking.

God sustained us.

City Life

When I moved to Los Angeles my major concern was transferring Nichol out of the Pasadena school system. Another concern I had was moving to such a large city. I suggested that Nichol stay with her dad until she graduated, and come to my house on the weekends. She was adamant about moving to Los Angeles with me.

Nichol was in the tenth grade when she left all her friends behind in Pasadena. The school she was assigned to attend was rough. Inglewood High School was a little bit out of her league. Nichol did not like the school at all, it reminded her of the movie "Lean on Me." She began ditching class and hanging out down the street at a burger stand.

By the time I found out about it she had been out of school for over a month. When the school office called me to come to the school, the truant officers took her out in handcuffs. She had to go continuation classes for the remainder of the year. I was in shock! I called my prayer warriors again, and we took our petition to the Lord. I asked God to give me direction, and an open door for her to attend a school in a better school district.

Once again God answered my prayer.

We had a meeting with the principal and counselor at the new school. Once they saw Nichol's transcripts they agreed to allow Nichol to attend there. Against my better judgment, I allowed Nichol to talk me into letting her change schools the following school year. She had a crush on a young brother at our church. His mother volunteered to drop them off and pick them up. That was a bad idea.

Nichol and the guy fell out while on a church outing and stopped speaking. There I was left with regret. Looking back in hindsight, that was the worst decision I could have made. She did not fit in there. We had no other choice than to ride out the year. She got off the basketball team because there were openly gay girls on the team. She was not used to going to school and being around that type of behavior. It made her very uncomfortable.

The only friends she had were at church. She could not wait for the weekend to come so she could attend church. The move to Los Angeles was quite an adjustment for Nichol. She was counting down the days for graduation.

Church Hurt

Nichol was very close to our Pastor's wife and family. I guess it would be fair to say, she was a little spoiled by them. The first lady showered Nichol with gifts. It was as though she had a second mother. In the beginning, I thought it was a good idea that Nichol spent time with her. She was an only child, and enjoyed being around a saved household.

Nichol was seventeen getting ready to graduate, and a student in Bible college. She was at the campus one night taking her finals. She called to let me know she was going over to choir rehearsal. Nichol was driving my car. She was always a responsible young lady, so I didn't have a problem letting her stay out. She always let me know where she was. Most of the time she was either at the church, or at the "saints" houses.

As the story was told to me by Nichol, she was in the fellowship hall talking with two of her childhood friends. They assumed they were alone, but someone overheard their conversation. Her fourteen year old friend shared with them that she had been having an affair with a married minister at our church. This young girl had been talking about this to my daughter for the past year. Nichol and the other young lady now took her seriously.

When they concluded their conversation all three of them went inside the sanctuary to watch the choir rehearse. The pastor was at the church in his office, and his wife was on the other side of the church in her office. Nichol said the first lady's office door suddenly swung open. The young minister that had been the topic of the conversation stood with his hands on his hips, and an angry look on his face.

As the choir sang, he motioned to the three teens to come into the office immediately. When they went in, the young minister, his pregnant wife, and the first lady were already present. The minister began questioning them in an accusing tone about what was said in the fellowship hall. They were in shock.

Nichol stormed out of the meeting and walked across the front of the church to notify the pastor. Once Nichol explained everything to him; he called his wife, and all involved to come into his office at once. The situation should have never been handled in the manner that it was. Nichol adamantly defended her friend insisting that the allegation needed to be investigated.

The pastor told his wife, "Be quiet and let Nichol speak." His wife was a little embarrassed that she was openly rebuked. That action would later cost Nichol big time. When she explained everything to the pastor, he looked over at the young girl and ask her one question, in a strong stern voice. "Is it true?" The pastor said.

The room was quiet.

The young lady was under a tremendous amount of pressure. All eyes were on her, as they all awaited the answer. She looked at the young minister. I can imagine that the air was so thick you could cut it with a knife. My daughter said the minister looked at her friend as though to say, 'Please don't tell.' It was her moment to tell the truth, but because of fear and her love for her abuser she covered up the truth. "No," she answered, timidly.

If anyone was holding their breath, they could now exhale.

The pastor told everyone to drop it, let it go, and don't even tell their parents. He did not want to hear any more about it. My Pastor tended to avoid confrontation, and sweep things under the carpet. Yet, he would preach over the pulpit putting people's business on blast causing public humiliation.

Good pastors can still make mistakes.

In the meantime, I was at home worried. I had not heard from Nichol, and wondered why she was not home yet.

Cell phones were not as common in those days, we both had pagers. I paged her, but she never responded. I tried to call the church; no answer. All I could do was wait for her to come home.

When Nichol finally came home she was so upset she could hardly talk. I kept asking her what happened. She had a blank stare on her face.

"Mom you're not going to believe it," Nichol said.

She wanted to take a shower first to calm her nerves, so she could tell me the story. Once she told me what happened I could not believe it myself. I was upset and wrestled with how to handle the situation; since the pastor said to drop it. I already had so much going on in my life. I was very fragile, and was not courageous enough to confront the pastor. I figured things would blow over as most situations did that occurred at our church, but not this time.

The Aftermath

After the incident, the pastor's family turned against Nichol. They took sides with the young minister, since he was like a son to the pastor. They did not want to believe he conducted himself in such a manner. He had been at the church since he was a teenager. Of course, the minister denied this accusation against him. I had been defending him the whole year prior to the incident, whenever my daughter shared with me that her friend claimed she was involved with young man. Now, I was not at all sure what to think.

When we went back to church the pastor's wife started mistreating Nichol. She was a beautiful woman, and adored by many. She was sweet most of the time, until you crossed her. She could be very controlling and manipulative. It reminded me of a mafia mentality. She had great influence on those close to her. Whatever she said, that's how it was. I thought that the relationship between Nichol and the first lady was strong enough to withstand opposition.

Nichol served as the first lady's armor bearer (assistant) escorting her into service. She also sat on, what was referred to as "the family row." Her position changed very quickly. The pastor's daughters also, began to shun Nichol. The pastor's wife even started to treat me rudely.

The next Sunday we came to church the first lady told Nichol she could no longer sit on "the family row." She also was removed as her armor bearer. Sometimes we got to church, and the usher would tell us there were no seats available. We would have to go sit in the balcony.

Prior to the drama, the pastor's family planned to attend Nichol's high school graduation. The school had only given her a certain amount of tickets. The first lady asked Nichol to save five tickets for their family. As graduation approached, she told her they were not going to make it. That was the straw that broke the camel's back. It was obvious we had been targeted.

I saw the first lady in the restroom during service. We were standing beside one another at the double-sinks. "Praise the Lord!" I said, cheerful. She stared into the mirror, flipped her long hair over her shoulder and never acknowledged me as she walked out. I stood there speechless.

Once you got on her hit list everyone else in power jumped on the bandwagon. It reminded me of how it was in school when your name was on the chalkboard for all to see. I recall Nichol's behavior started to change. She seemed sad because of everything that was going on, but I thought she would eventually be alright.

The rejection of being kicked off the family row discouraged her. The fact that none of them attended her graduation pierced her to the heart. It was devastating to say the least. Nichol waited for a phone call, but never received one.

After graduation, Nichol started to stay home from church. She did not have a desire to go. She had never missed church, it was her life. I'm talking about a girl that did everything involving church. She attended concerts, trips, and teen retreats. I thought maybe she just needed a breather.

Graduation Day w/ Grandma Wyatt

Dr. Iona Locke

Prom Night

Nichol came to church a few times after taking a break, but was treated with the same disdain. On one New Year's Eve Communion Service, we arrived a little late because I had to work. I told Nichol to ask the usher to sit her on the family row. As I watched the usher escort Nichol to the "the family row," the gesture of the first lady's body language told it all. Pastor's wife held her hand up and vehemently shook her head 'NO' stating, "She cannot sit here." There was an offensive disposition that I saw from where I stood. It was horrible. It broke my heart. We were about to take communion, "The Lord's Supper," and her attitude was this nasty?

We both ended up in the balcony oppressed in a service that was supposed to be joyful. We left church feeling defeated. Eventually, Nichol stopped coming to church altogether. I believe what hurt her most, is the fact that neither our pastor nor his family ever called her.

One hug could have changed her life.

Before long Nichol became distant. I started noticing a change in her friends. One day I found a container of alcohol in the trunk of my car. It was left in an unfamiliar backpack. When I asked Nichol who it belonged to, she told me she gave a friend a ride.

"They must have left it in the car mom," She said.

I had no reason to believe otherwise, since Nichol was not the type of girl that was known to be a liar. Shortly after that I found a marijuana cigarette on her bedroom floor. Again, she had an excuse of where that came from. Her pattern of behavior became unpredictable.

Next, she started showing up late to pick me up from work in 'my car.' She started having one excuse after the other. Months had passed since she had attended church. Meantime, she turned eighteen, and I gradually lost control over her decision making. We were not connecting like we had been. I was angry at her most of the time. I could not put my finger on what was wrong.

Ultimately, the minister accused of messing with Nichol's under aged friend was exposed. His own wife found a letter from the girl. What took place between them sexually nobody knows but God. Whatever truth had come to light did not affect Nichol's decision to live so carelessly.

I would say to any parent, to pay attention when your children are transitioning from adolescence to adulthood. Behavior or appearance may be a sign that something is wrong. Someone asked one day, did I notice any changes in her attire or mannerisms. When I think about it, Nichol was never one to dress provocatively. Even as a young girl she did not like her sleeves out or short pants.

As I reflected back when Nichol was a teenager, the loose-fitting, cartoon button-down shirts were in style. All the teens in her circle were wearing them. Then the basketball jerseys came out that had the teams on them. Also, name brand tennis shoes were trending. The hip-hop attire seemed to be the movement.

Nichol was a tomboy in her early years, I did not think much of it. I attributed it to my own background. I had eight brothers, and was a tomboy coming up myself. I figured she would grow out of it. On Sunday mornings, she wore suits and heels, with designer bags to match.

More and more strange incidents began to occur, and more frequently I might add. Her friends became stranger by the day. I did not know these people with names like Savoya and Coco. I assumed she was trying to persuade them into going to church. I was clueless. Why else would she be hanging out with such worldly people? These were not the type of friends that Nichol had ever been around. I had no idea she was acting up out of rejection.

These weird women came by to pick Nichol up to go "somewhere" for a weekend. The whole thing troubled me. Nichol had never done anything like this before. I did not know what to think. She was always around me or with the church family. These people seemed a little wild. They were in a convertible car, and just looked very worldly. One had on a long wig, the other had a blonde bob cut. They both appeared to be much older than Nichol.

The whole scene was scary. I was deeply concerned. Nichol painted the picture as though she was growing up, and trying to get over her "church hurt." She claimed she was having a little fun with her new circle of friends.

As a mother, I felt very alarmed. Nichol jumped into the convertible and waved goodbye. They drove off into the sunset. I stood on the front porch staring down the street, as the Devil drove off with my baby. I later found out that these "two worldly women" were actually men. Back in my day we referred to cross-dressers as "drag queens."

Nichol always had thick, beautiful, shoulder-length hair. She decided she wanted to cut it. I felt in my Spirit there was something wrong. When you know your child, you sense these things. Nichol just was not the type to be that daring to chop off her hair so drastically. I hesitantly cut a few inches, but she wanted more chopped off. I cut it to the top of her ears in a short bob.

The next thing I noticed she slightly changed her attire. I thought she was just transitioning from high school clothing to young adulthood. Turning eighteen is an awkward age. I figured she was trying to get a sense of her own style.

Then, a few weeks later she decided she wanted to go a little shorter, and put blonde in her hair. I knew then, this is going somewhere. I was still not quite sure where. I became a little nervous, but after all she was considered an adult making her own choices. I guess I was trying to figure out exactly what was going on with her. We always talked about any and everything. Now it appeared she was turning a deaf ear to me.,

I had so much going on in my own life, I was not in tune. Normally I would have paid more attention to these types of signs. I recently had been through a divorce from my husband of almost twenty years. My life was completely turned upside down. I relocated to a new city. We had to move twice within two years.

I felt the pressure of becoming a single parent. After being accustomed to having two pay checks, I now operated on one income. More responsibilities weighed on me, which caused my focus not to be on Nichol as much. During all this, my baby brother passed away.

Nichol was supposed to be headed to college. I was expecting an empty nest real soon. I figured she would come home to visit on Thanksgiving and Christmas. I had great expectations for Nichol's future.

Nichol occasionally went with me to visit other churches. I tried desperately to keep her interested in the Lord. Once she experienced the hurt in church, she could never seem to get back in the flow. She drifted far away from her spiritual foundation. Her associates got weirder and weirder.

I received a call from a friend of Nichol's. She attended another church in a city about four hours away. She was so upset, she was in tears.

"What is wrong. Are you okay?" I asked.

"I have to tell you something," she said.

"Sure, go ahead honey," I replied.

"Nichol has confided in me that she thinks she's gay," she said.

"What! Are you sure? I asked, puzzled.

I was floored, but I also thought possibly the friend had misunderstood her. I figured, Nichol must be going through a phase from being hurt at church. Why would she tell this young lady something like this? I could not piece this puzzle together.

When Nichol came home I told her all about the conversation I had with her friend. She tried to avoid having this discussion. Nichol was confused, and a bit embarrassed to admit she was struggling with these feelings.

51

"Do you think you're gay?" I asked.

"I'm not sure. I went to a club called 'Peanuts' in Hollywood with some girls I met. I had a few drinks and a girl kissed me," Nichol said, nervously.

I was trying to be the understanding "Mom" that I had portrayed to be all these years. I proceeded to reason with her.

My faith was now on trial.

I don't think she was ready to talk to me about it just yet. She seemed very uncomfortable. She was also angry that her friend shared this information with me. I wanted to help. As a parent we feel it's our job to fix things. Nichol and I were always able to talk about anything. I raised her to be very open with me. I wanted her to feel comfortable to come to me about anything. Ultimately, I discovered later, the friend that spilled the beans from church had engaged in lesbian acts with Nichol.

I attributed her experimental mindset as the result of the rejection she had encountered at church. I thought to myself, 'she's confused, she's angry, and we are going to talk through this.' I thought it was something we could deal with in prayer. I surely did not think it was going to become so extreme. Well, this issue ended up taking me down a road of heartache and tears.

Nichol became progressively distant toward me. She was disengaged from spiritual things altogether. She barely came home. I felt that I had lost my influence. Eventually, Nichol shut completely down on me. I felt hopeless.

Remember Job in the Old Testament? He was perfect, upright, feared God, and shunned evil. Job offered burnt offerings on behalf of his children continually. Satan is always seeking for an opportunity to torment our life. I had done all that I could to secure a bright outcome for Nichol's life. Instead, the Devil slipped in on my watch.

Disappearing Act

I came home from work one day only to discover all my daughter's belongings were gone. I contacted my ex-husband to see if he had heard from her. At that point she did not have a lot of close friends, especially friends she would disappear with. He told me she had moved back to Pasadena to live with him. I noticed a few changes in her behavior, but I certainly was not grasping the severity of it.

Apparently, I had been in denial as to the magnitude and significance her sudden character changes, and appearance which had taken place.

She had recently graduated from high school. I really thought she was on her way to college to begin her life as an adult. I had no idea why she would abruptly pick up and move out without notifying me. We had differences before, but nothing major. We always worked it out.

I got in my car and headed to my ex-husband's house. As I drove there I was pondering what had brought all this on. I asked myself, 'Why would she have to move out?' It made no sense.

I arrived at the house. As I walked in the front door my ex-husband met me at the bottom of the stairs.
"You might want to sit down," he said.
"Why would I need to sit down?" I asked.
"You might not be ready for this," Jack said.

He had the strangest expression on his face. At that moment, I was not quite sure what I was about to encounter. He yelled up the stairs for Nichol to come down.
"Your mom is here," he said.

Nichol walked down the stairs, my heart skipped a beat. While watching her come from the top of the steps I almost passed out. I thought I was having a heart attack. I

53

gasped for breath, as I grabbed my chest. I could hardly believe what I was seeing. I squinted my eyes because I was trying to recognize "this person."

There was someone else coming down those stairs. Literally, overnight, she had completely changed her entire appearance. Her beautiful hair was shaved off into a bald fade haircut. She had on a big sloppy boy's shirt, a sports bra, and oversized baggy pants.

I was looking at her in disbelief. I stared from the top of her head, down to those boy tennis shoes on her feet. I later realized she even changed underwear to boy's boxers, and tee-shirts… the whole nine. As she reached the bottom of the stairs she was not walking the same. Her walk was even masculine. Her attitude was boldly making a declaration. I did not know what to say.

"Do you want to sit down? Would you like some water? You okay? Jack asked, concerned.

I could barely talk. I didn't know what to think. I didn't know what to say. I was speechless.

"What are you doing? What is going on?" I asked.

"Hey Mom, this is what I'm doing right now." Nichol replied, firmly. "I'm going to be staying with Dad for now," she said.

Everything was so foggy, as if I this was a bad dream. It was like an evil spirit had taken over my daughter. Her demeanor was that of a mannish, rebellious, teenage boy.

She was absolute about what it was she decided to walk into. Without any discussion? Just like that! At that moment I was in a daze. Nichol turned around nonchalantly, and proceeded back upstairs. I considered what she was wearing to be a ridiculous costume. I was completely floored. I felt like a total failure as a parent. Time stood still.

I drove home with tears streaming down my face. I was in utter disbelief. Of course, the enemy being the accuser that he is, started talking to me. 'What have I done wrong? Where did I go wrong? How could this have happened? She was with me all the time. Maybe I should not have moved to the inner-city.'

The Devil had taken my beautiful little girl that I invested my life into. She had been tricked into becoming someone God did not ordain for her to be. Nichol was deceived by the enemy into embracing a lifestyle of homosexuality. She made the choice to take a walk on the dark side. A walk that would end up costing her twenty years of her life. The Bible says, "Be sober, be vigilant; because your adversary the devil, as a roaring lion, walks about seeking whom he may devour" (1Peter 5:8 KJV).

Cut her hair off at 18 the Devil Stole my Innocent Baby

State of Shock

I woke up the next morning feeling helpless, and drained. I barely could get out of bed. I reached out to my prayer warrior sisters in Christ. These women were a close group of friends at my church. We often came together in prayer, fasting, and Bible study. When any of us faced a crisis, we supported each other.

These friends had known Nichol since a child. One of the women was at the altar praying with her when she received the Holy Ghost. They encouraged me and prayed for me concerning what I was going through with Nichol. I never would have imagined in a thousand years that my life would have gone this way. Nobody could have prophesied to me what was ahead. Nichol's decision to explore the gay lifestyle turned my life into shambles.

Nichol's move to Pasadena did not last long. Her Dad lived about 30 minutes outside of Los Angeles. That was too far from the clubs she became so intrigued with. She eventually moved back home, and used it as a flop house.

Clothed in Shame

I was so embarrassed. I was crushed. I kept thinking, not my daughter. Of course, I talked to God, but the feelings of despair were so great. I was not even sure if my prayers were being heard. I had been through so much already. I was hoping for a reprieve. Now this?

At this point, I felt as though I was going from one trial to another. It seems as though I could not get a break or even catch my breath. It was so overwhelming. I had not been this way before. Usually I was a strong woman. My faith and my belief in God was solid. This situation was shaking my foundation.

This thing right here, was more than I wanted to handle. If only "this cup" ... could pass from me. The only way I could describe it is, I felt like I was in a time warp. It was the Twilight Zone for sure. This could not be happening to me. I raised her in church.

The warfare was intense, and I had to get armored up.

One day, I was at work in the salon busy doing my clients hair. Two young ladies walked in. When they came to my station, they noticed a picture of Nichol. It was a picture of her in a church dress wearing a fancy hat. To my surprise they recognized her, but they called her by a street name. They chuckled among themselves.

"We know her," one lady said.

They were amused that she had on a dress and church hat. It was obvious that the girls were gay from their attire. The two of them were a lesbian couple. It was clear by how they interacted with one another. I felt nervous. I thought, 'Oh my God, what are they getting ready to say about my daughter?'

"That's Jamil, how do you know her?" they asked.

"That's my daughter," I responded.

I'm wondering, how do they know her? Jamil? 'Who in the world is Jamil?' I was so embarrassed. I hoped no one in the salon heard them. My heart sunk.

The two girls spoke in a sort of taunting voice. They did not care that the picture of my daughter was at my private station. That devil held nothing back, and used them to try to expose the fact that Nichol ran in the same circle as they did. "Gay circles," that is. I hurried up and finished their service to get them out of there. After the girls left, I took the picture off my station. It was apparent that Nichol was not being discreet about her new lifestyle.

Sometimes, when I got off from work I walked across the parking lot to the grocery store. I saw a mother and daughter together shopping, and I got so sad. I missed my baby girl. We had been so close all her life.

Seems as though everything changed overnight. It was hard to adjust to the separation, everything reminded me of the things we did together. I found myself feeling very lonely. I experienced so many different emotions. I cried often.

She was an innocent church girl, and the next thing I knew she was out in the street life. A life I so desperately worked hard to keep her away from. I began to weep uncontrollably. I had to leave the store.

The enemy continually plagued my mind. I started to beat myself up. Not only was I devastated by the choices Nichol made, I was embarrassed. I felt like her choices reflected on me as being a bad parent. All these thoughts constantly ran through my mind like a broken record. "How did this happen? Where did I go wrong?" I raised her in church, not just any church. I raised her in an Apostolic (holiness) church. This was not supposed to happen, I replayed everything in my mind constantly.

Nichol was not forced to go to church, she loved going. Pastor preached the whole Bible, and taught against all sin. Nichol knew that homosexuality was a detestable sin. Yet, she chose to go that route.

I tried my best to remain optimistic. I told myself it was "just a phase." It's the 21st Century, I reasoned within myself...I thought 'well, people try things now days, like they try a new hairstyle. Maybe this was something that would be short lived.' Since Nichol lived with me, I felt I could just talk her out of this. I was hoping to convince her that this was something she did not want to get involved in.

I knew my daughter's decision to live a gay lifestyle would cause a separation from the presence of God. This choice would take her straight to hell if she did not repent. Unbeknownst to me, Nichol dropped out of college. I saw her less and less. I could not reach her. I felt as though she was a stranger in my house. I was disappointed in her choices.

There was constant friction between the two of us. She was determined to live the way she wanted to live, without hearing my opinion. Nichol became stubborn and rebellious. I recall trying to have a conversation with Nichol in our kitchen.

"Are you having a nervous breakdown?" I asked.

Nichol did not answer me.

"Have you lost your damn mind," I screamed.

I was furious, and had lost my composure! I had not used profanity in years.

She just looked at me with a foolish expression. She made me so angry I grabbed a knife, and chased her out the back door. We never interacted this way. Nichol was not a disobedient teenager prior to all this. Her new personality was draining.

I was so distraught. Two friends stopped by to pray with me the following day. I shared with them what happened. Sister Kay suggested that we anoint Nichol's room as an act of faith, believing that the presence of God would rest in her room. We went into her room and anointed the door post and windows. Sister Alicia recommended that we get on our knees and stretch across her bed to pray over it. The three of us placed anointing oil on all Nichol's belongings and prayed as well. At that moment I knew God heard my prayer. I felt encouraged.

Strategy Change

After much prayer and fasting I was led to take a different approach with Nichol. The lifestyle she chose began to alter my entire life. This is not how it was supposed to go. We made it to the finish line, but Nichol fumbled the ball. I had so many expectations for her. She was well supported by both sides of the family.

My daughter was such an intelligent young lady. She had a 3.8 GPA, and could have gone to any college of her choice. I later found out that she had even skipped the SAT test when I dropped her off to take the exam. Nichol had no intention of going to college.

Nichol lied about different things out of fear of what I might say. She was now eighteen, considered to be an adult. By law there really was nothing I could do. We had many discussions about her life now that she had made this decision to come out of "the closet." It didn't appear to me that she had a plan. Those were conversations she tried to avoid by any means necessary. She was always getting dressed on the phone, or locked in her room.

Nichol stayed busy, doing God knows what, with God knows who, and God knows where. Sometimes, I would sit in the living room waiting to hear from her. Days would pass by before she called home. Even though she was considered grown, I still worried about her. It had only been a few months ago she was my little girl that I was picking up after school.

The enemy would start to play with my mind. Satan would have me thinking 'Someone is going to kill her, or something terrible is going to happen to her.'
"Loose here Satan, the blood of Jesus!" I said, aloud.

One year in Los Angeles we had a very bad storm called "El Niño." We never got a lot of storms in Southern California, but this one was bad. I sat on my chaise lounge reading my Bible. I was praying, reading, and crying. I had no idea if my child was okay out in that weather. I was hoping that Nichol would walk up those red stairs leading to our front door, but she did not come. Not that day.

I went to bed, but I could not sleep. I could not focus, I was tormented. I questioned the Lord, "How in the world did this happen? What is going on? How long is this going to last? Lord this seems too much to bare."

The same questions were playing over and over in my mind. It got so bad, I started to prepare for the worst. I thought she was going to die young. The way that Nichol digressed so abruptly; I accepted the fact that she would not live long.

When Nichol eventually showed up, I would be so happy to see her. I would try to do all I could to keep her in the house. Her demeanor was completely different now. It was obvious that she was doing some type of drug. I was so accommodating that she took total of advantage of that. I was always fearful that she would leave again and be gone for days.

I cooked her food, washed her clothes, and made up her bed trying to keep her comfortable at home. Soon as the phone rang she would be out the door. Oftentimes she would come home, and I would turn the ringer off hiding her phone. Nichol looked run down from days of partying, and was so exhausted that she slept for hours.

Though I was disappointed, I had compassion for her. It was sad to see such a gifted young lady throwing her life away. Here was a girl that was a pretty good kid. Don't get me wrong, she did her little mischievous pranks growing up. The main problem she had was joking, and talking too much in class. This new behavior was very abnormal.

I realized I needed to take a different approach. Fussing was not working, nor pleading, or bombarding her with scripture. When she turned a deaf ear to the word of God, my heart broke. This warfare could not be won in my flesh.

The Lord let me know I needed to show her love in spite of her choices. I thought maybe if I tried to understand what she was going through; this test would be over soon. I did not want to appear that I was compromising my beliefs or condoning her actions. It was very difficult to work through this process. I prayed for direction. The Bible says, *"If any man lack wisdom to ask of God who gives to all men liberally and upbraideth not"* (James 1:5 KJV).

It was time for me to go into serious spiritual warfare! It was clear that the enemy was not going to let my baby girl go easily. I had to put my pity parties aside and realize I was going to have to fight for my daughter's deliverance. The war was on. I realized that Satan was targeting me in an attempt to distract me from ministry.

Once Nichol felt comfortable that I was in her corner she let her guard down a little bit. I let her know I was not going to give up on her. The Lord had invested too much. I constantly reminded her of God's love, and also how much I loved her. I could not listen to too many opinions. I had to go straight to the throne of God. I was in an unfamiliar territory. I had been around others living the homosexual lifestyle, but not right in my face like this. As I continued to pray and fast, the Lord began to deal with me on how to approach or tackle the spirit of homosexuality.

"Love the person, hate the sin. It's just like ministering to anyone else that is overtaken in sin. You 'must' show love to your daughter," the Holy Spirit spoke softly to me.

The Officer Didn't Impound her friend's car

The Word Was Out

News like this spread quickly, especially in the church circles. I began to get phone calls from various people in other churches. Nichol was very popular in a large Pentecostal Organization. We frequently attended the church conventions. Nichol was also active in various teen activities around the city such as Bible Bowl (training for scripture debate).

Nichol was the first woman to be appointed on the security team at our church. When we went to the church councils she sat with the first lady on the row that was designated for pastor's wives. Since she would be with her so often, she met a lot of Bishops and their wives. I was glad she was interested in the things of God. The tables sure had turned.

I received a phone call from one of Nichol's Bible college instructors. He was a pastor at another church, and had gotten wind of Nichol's new transition. He asked me if he could take her to breakfast and try to talk some sense into her. I desperately agreed. They went to breakfast, but it was not successful. Nichol was hurt and angry. The people she wanted to hear from never called from that day until now. She was waiting on Pastor and his wife to reach out, but it never happened.

Some of her play aunts from the church, and a few of the young people reached out to her. That did not have any impact. As time went by the members began to miss her presence in service. Many asked about her and were genuinely concerned. There was one Mother of the church named Mother Pinks that consistently called and relayed messages through me to Nichol.

"Hello, Praise the Lord!" I answered.

"Praise the Lord." Mother Pinks replied, in her frail, soft voice. "How's my girl doing?" she asked.

"She's okay Mother," I sighed. "Please keep praying for her. I'm trying to remain optimistic," I said.

"Tell her I called, and that I love her, I'm praying for her and I want to see her face at church soon, okay?" She said.

"Yes ma'am, thank you so much, I appreciate it, I will let her know you called."

Most of the time she was not at home when the calls came. I would relay the messages to her, I got no response.

Nichol was riding the city bus one afternoon and the driver was from our church. She tried to exit out the rear back door, but the woman locked her on the bus. She forced Nichol to exit up front, so that she could confirm that it was her. That following Sunday the Devil used this woman to embarrass me.

"Oh my gosh Sister Yevette! I saw your daughter looking like a boy. What's going on? Her hair is bald, and she is wearing men's clothes," she said, in a loud sarcastic tone.

"Just pray for her," I said, walking off.

I got to my car and cried on the way home. Not once did she say she was praying. I was not close to her at all. It seemed to me if she was genuinely concerned she would have used discretion opposed to blurting it out. The Devil used that lady.

Even my neighbors were looking at me side-eyed now. I had witnessed to most of the people on my street. They had been seeing my daughter for years before her drastic transition. Nichol was sweetly saved waving at them often as we left for church. It seemed like overnight she was with a bald fade, boy's clothes, and sagging pants.

My co-workers saw my daughter walking around in the neighborhood, and they were not accustomed to seeing her look like day and night. They asked very concerned if she was okay. All I could say was my daughter chose an alternative lifestyle.

Anywhere but Home
Santa Monica Blvd.

There came a time that Nichol did not want to be at home at all. She began to hang out on Santa Monica Blvd. at a 24-hour donut shop. This was a whole other way of life that Nichol was not accustomed to. It appeared she was spiraling into the abyss.

For the life of me I could not understand why she wanted to be up there. It was a lot going on. Packs of people standing around on the street corners, and pacing the boulevard all night. It was like a nighttime parade. This environment looked like a freak show.

Nichol would sometimes call me when she needed me. I made so many drives up a familiar street in Los Angeles called Highland. I was afraid for her. I wanted her to come home. We could have put all this craziness behind us, and started over as though nothing ever happened. Once I arrived, Nichol would not get in the car. She was living like a run away without parents.

Nichol always had her own room at home. There was a nice comfortable bed, and TV. Why would anyone in their right mind want to live on the streets? One day, Nichol came to the house with some of her so called "friends." We had the worst fight. I believe this was the first time Nichol ever disrespected me.

She was literally turning into another person before my very eyes. I was in shock. My heart was crushed. She stormed out the door and stood on the porch to give me a piece of her mind. She left with some strangers. If anything happened, I would not know where to look or who it was she had left with.

Another occasion, she brought home a young Spanish girl. The girl was sloppy drunk with tattoos all over her face and body. Her head was shaved completely like with a razor. It was a sad sight to witness. Nichol felt sorry for her. She told me that the girl was living on the streets, and they met on Santa Monica Blvd. She looked like a hard-core lil' cholo boy.

At that time, I realized that being a Christian was more than dressing up in a suit and hat. It was not just about sitting in a comfortable church with air conditioning and soft pews. I heard the Lord say, "Feed her." I looked around the room, "What Lord," I replied. Again, the voice said, "Feed her." The girl could hardly stand up.

Next thing I knew she had passed out on my practically new sofa. I'm thinking 'What's becoming of my life?' I was obedient when she awoke, I gave her something to eat. Nichol told the Spanish girl that I was an Evangelist if she needed to talk or wanted prayer.

Periodically, Nichol would call with a friend on the phone that needed advice, or bring someone by the house for prayer. God began to give me compassion for the wayward young people that crossed Nichol's path. She knew Holiness was right, though she chose not to adhere to the lifestyle. Nichol was clueless to the fact that she was operating in the capacity of an outreach minister.

Nichol plummeted deeper and deeper into sin. I received another call from a young lady named Keisha that also was a lesbian. She called herself Nichol's play sister. Keisha was concerned about Nichol's safety. Nichol was renting a hotel in Hollywood selling drugs. One of the guys told Keisha that my daughter stuck out like a sore thumb. He wondered what she was doing up there because she did not fit in. Nichol was articulate, and neat in her appearance. He told Keisha to come down town.

Nichol's life was at constant risk. She had no clue how dangerous it was to live in the streets at that point. She seemed to want fast money. She was intrigued with the street life. God was so merciful, He protected Nichol in her ignorance. I was afraid that I would receive a phone call that something awful happened to my child. She was so destructive and careless, like she had no fear of death.

False Alarm

Early on in Nichol's quest to live a backslidden life, she called to tell me she met a "guy." I thought, 'Ah, yes my nightmare is short lived.' I was relieved. I felt like whew, as I exhaled. I remember hoping for sure this is the "cure all." The young man was not saved. I had not met him yet, but "at least he's a man," I said to myself.

One morning, months later, she confessed to me that she had her first sexual encounter with this guy. You would think since I am an evangelist and prayer warrior I would have been furious. Under ordinary circumstances, I would have started pleading the blood of Jesus. To be perfectly honest, I was so desperate, it seemed like good news to me.

I was convicted in my spirit that I was applauding sin. I was humanly happy that at least she was going to be with the opposite sex. I called a good friend of mine. She was also an evangelist, I might add. I shared the "great news" with her. She was excited.

"I know we should not be rejoicing about sin, but I don't want to see you hurt anymore. This might be the one to turn her around," she said.

"I sure hope so girl," I replied.

I figured, since Nichol was already backslidden this would bring her back to church in some sort of odd way. I was thinking maybe she could repent for everything all at one time. Sin is deceitful. I convinced myself Nichol was going to snap out of it. However, this saga was just beginning.

This was Nichol's first intimate relationship with a man, and it took her by storm. Shortly afterward, she was spending lots of time with him. I met him a few times. At least I knew where she was now.

Nichol called in tears one day. I felt helpless, I wanted to rescue her. She was constantly in turmoil. There were several incidents of domestic violence between her and the young man. Nichol stuck around through the abuse. If she insisted on staying, it was nothing I could do. I put my Trust in God. I relied on my faith to see her through. I fell to my knees and prayed.

My dreams were shattered. Sin never has positive results. The love affair did not last long. I felt like an idiot. My judgment was compromised. I went against all that I knew to be right. I had to repent. God help!

Once Nichol cut ties with her abusive boyfriend, believe it or not she was not finished with sin. The abusive relationship caused her to become bitter. She became hard. She sunk even deeper into a life of perversion.

Jack is Back

Although, my ex-husband Jack was responsible for our marriage ending, he could not come to grips that it was over. We had been divorced for about three years. He was miserable. Since Jack and I had a peaceful divorce, we remained friends. Out of the blue, I got a call from him.

"Hello." I answered.

"Hey." He replied, in a deep baritone voice.

"What's going on?" I asked.

"You need to come home," Jack said.

"Are you kidding me? We have been divorced for three years now," I said, in amusement.

It was obvious that Jack wanted to reconcile. That was never something I considered. He remained hopeful. Jack was a likable guy, and it's fair to say he was also a pretty good provider. He had a problem with fidelity so our marriage could not survive.

Ironically, my Pastor asked about Jack the same day. I was at noon day Bible study. Afterward, I met with him to get Godly advice about my daughter Nichol. At the close of our meeting he asked me how Jack was doing?

"Have you heard from him lately?" Pastor asked.

I thought, 'Wow! I cannot believe he's asking about Jack.'

"As a matter of fact, he called me today," I answered.

"Oh, he did." Pastor said.

As if he expected that response.

"Yes, he had the nerve, to tell me to stop all this foolishness and come home," I said, sarcastically.

Pastor did not find any humor in my responses at all. I went on to relay the rest of the conversation. After all, I'm the one that had the upper hand on Jack. I assumed, not only is Pastor going to hear me out, but he's definitely going to agree with me. Jack ruined the marriage with his shenanigans. I felt entitled to refuse after all he put me through.

"Pastor, do you know what Jack had the nerve to say to me? He wants to come to church. I told Jack it's your church too, nobody is stopping you from coming," I said.

"Go get the man!" Pastor sternly responded.

I was surprised at Pastor's response.

"What? Go get him?" I said.

I was not expecting that. We were having evening Bible Study in a few hours. I could not believe Pastor told me to go get Jack. I set myself up for that one. Nonetheless, I would never stop someone from coming to church.

As I walked to my car in the church parking lot I stopped to use the payphone. I called my ex-husband. I wanted to be obedient to my pastor. I was genuinely concerned about Jack being spiritually re-connected to the Lord. As a minister of the gospel that was always my priority.

Jack answered the phone, I told him what happened in the pastor's office that day. Here was his big chance, I'm sure that's what was going through his mind. Jack was a good actor, especially if it was going to benefit him. His car was conveniently out of commission.

"Do you want to come to Bible study tonight?" I asked.

"Pastor asked me to pick you up," I said.

"Yes," Jack said, in a deep, low pitiful voice.

I must have been crazy! To agree to drive all the way from Carson to Pasadena in rush hour traffic. On a good day it was a forty-five minute drive. Jack went on to plead his case.

"I'll make you something to eat," he offered.

I have always loved his cooking; besides that, I had been at the church most of the day and was starving. Off I went.

I finally arrived at the house. The house I moved out of after our divorce. Jack had everything packed and eager to go. If only he had been this eager to come to church with me when we were married. He seemed desperate for change.

When we got to church Jack inhaled and exhaled slowly. He could be so dramatic. As we walked up the stairs to the front entrance Jack was so relieved. I never saw him act like that about going to church. It was strange. It was always such a struggle for him before. He rebelled against holy living, and did not allow God to perfect him through His word.

Bible Study had not started yet. The members began to come in and take their seats. As we stood in the vestibule of the church, one of my friends approached Jack to greet him. She met Jack a few years before our divorce. She was so glad to see him at church. No doubt she was surprised that he was there with me.

A few of the ushers remembered Jack. They were happy to see him. Jack hugged the ushers as though they were his "good friends." As we walked in sanctuary to take our seat, Jack was really putting on the Ritz. He was hugging anyone who remembered him.

Now this is the kicker! The ritual at my home church is to kneel in prayer before taking your seat. When we finally reached our seats, Jack bowed down, stretched out his arms across the pews, took a long deep breath with his eyes closed, and belted out a sigh of relief. He appeared to be at peace. I didn't know what to make of it. I was speechless.

Maybe he had an epiphany. He stayed down there so long I wondered if he had dropped dead. It would serve him right, coming back three years after our divorce was completely final. Imagine that, putting on a scene to win me back. He could have won the academy award that night for sure.

Bible Study was good as usual. Pastor was a phenomenal teacher/preacher, and all-around bible scholar. Afterward, Jack headed straight to Pastor. The two of them embraced. Pastor always liked Jack, even though he did not show up regularly.

"Praise the Lord Jack!" Pastor said, in excitement!

"Praise the Lord Pastor," Jack said, very humbly.

The two of them talked for a while. I took a seat and allowed Jack to fellowship with the few people that remembered him. It was a long day. I was overwhelmed. I drove Jack back home, and dropped him off. Whew!

I told Nichol about her Dad coming to Bible Study. As Sunday approached, Jack called to ask if I could pick him up once again for Sunday morning service. His car was still broke. Nichol agreed to go with me to get him. At the time we lived halfway between Jack's house and the church.

When we got to church Nichol sat in the balcony. Jack and I sat on the main floor of the sanctuary. We all went to dinner after service. Jack was so nice and polite. I had no intention on falling for any of his tricks. I had my eye on him.

Jack's All In

By the next Sunday Jack's car was fixed, and he drove himself to church. Pastor gave the altar call, which is the invitation for those that wanted to receive salvation or prayer. Jack got up without hesitation. He decided to rededicate his life back to God.

Service was on fire! The anointing was flowing. The saints were shouting and praising the Lord! Pastor looked over the pulpit and saw Jack. The look on Pastor's face said it all. He was ecstatic!

"Hallelujah!" Pastor screamed!

"The prodigal son has come home," he yelled!

The church went up in an uproar! There was an explosion of energy in the place. Pastor beckoned for his wife Earline to come work with Jack. "Work," refers to praying with him to be refreshed in the Spirit by speaking with other tongues.

Sister Earline began to minister to Jack. I could hardly believe what I was witnessing. My ex-husband is at the altar crying out to God with all his might. God's ways are truly past finding out. Why couldn't he surrender three years ago? I took a seat on the front row in amazement, as I watched Jack go through deliverance. He cried, he rolled on the floor. He spoke in tongues. The church went crazy with excitement! The prodigal son was home. My God.

I was happy for him as a brother in Christ that he wanted to come back to the Lord. Jack had been baptized in Jesus name and filled with the Holy Ghost some years prior. Back then he only came to church four Sundays and got discouraged and quit going. He never developed a relationship with God.

The following Sunday Jack came to church on his own. He was like a newborn babe. Little did I know Jack had a plan to get his wife back. Most of the congregation did not even know Jack and I were divorced. Some referred to him as "your husband." Many gave congratulations to me for "my husband's" restoration. I was constantly explaining myself.

"He's not my husband." I repeatedly defended my position. Various members began to say, "It's a miracle that God brought your husband back."

I constantly had to remind them "he's not my husband." I'm glad God brought him back, but he's not for me. I hope he finds someone, but I am not his wife. It took much healing and deliverance to get over Jack. I was ready to move on. I felt I had wasted enough years trying to perfect my marriage.

An Evangelist from my church came into the salon to get her hair done. She too was bit by the 'Jack bug.'

"Can't you see this is a miracle? God brought your husband back! Are you all going to get remarried?" She asked.

"No!" I firmly replied.

"Why not?" The evangelist asked.

For one thing, I had gone through tremendous opposition to get the courage to leave Jack, whom I loved. I met him when I was twenty-two, at a tough time in my life. It took some time to get over him, and the disappointment of a failed marriage in the church.

During Jack's restoration, I was still going through challenges with my daughter's predicament. Several people were determined to convince me that Jack's return to church was nothing short of a miracle. I hoped that Jack's decision might influence Nichol to return to God also.

My joy was in Jesus. I was in love with Jesus and He loved me. My strength came from attending church. I was at church all day on Sunday. I attended Sunday School through Sunday evening service. Monday nights, I was an assistant at Prayer. Wednesdays, I went to afternoon and evening Bible Study. Friday, I attended ministerial services, and Saturday once a month Women's Prayer.

I also attended our yearly women's retreats, church conferences, and had fellowship wherever I could find a gathering. I kept myself occupied under the anointing and presence of God to maintain my sanity. Otherwise these burdens would have been too heavy to carry. I often to reminded myself of the scripture, "He will never put any more on you than you can bear."

Nichol continued full speed ahead. She was determined to prove a point that she was going to be her own person, and call her own shots. I was going through the motions of day-to-day life, trying to function. I still experienced intense emotional pain and very seldom got any relief. So many things were going on in my personal life; my daughter backslid, my baby brother had recently passed away, I was under attack at work, and some of my closest friendships are being tried. I was looking for a recess.

I called my pastor, once again, to get advice concerning Nichol. I can't even recall what transpired, but I was in tears when I made the call to him. Pastor was so saddened that I was upset. He figured the best thing was to inquire what my ex-husband Jack thought about it.
"What is Jack saying?" Pastor Art said.
"I don't know, he just wants to get remarried, he wants his wife back," I cried.

Pastor wanted the whole thing over with. He really didn't have much patience when it came to matters of the heart. He believed wholeheartedly in the reconciliation of family. He would become overwhelmed if you cried in front of hom. He could not take a woman in tears. He would agree with you quick just to stop the tears.
"Well, what are you waiting on? Just marry the man!" Pastor said.
My cry instantly turned into a whimper.

"Huh?" I sniffled as I gathered my emotions.

"Marry him?" I questioned.

"Yes, I feel this is the right thing to do. Jack has come back to church and given his life back to the Lord. I just don't think that Jack would come back and mess up this time Sister Yevette," Pastor said.

I paused in silence.

"Okay, thanks, goodbye Pastor," I said, sadly.

I began to replay previous conversations I had with church members concerning Jack's restoration. I was emotionally, spiritually, and mentally unstable. At that point I was spiritually bankrupt. I was going through so much, and it appeared as though it was never going to end. My only child spiraling out of control, and I had recently lost one of my baby brothers.

I felt like I was in the twelfth round of a boxing match, and I was losing. I was dazed. I was not in any condition to be making serious decisions. During this period, I was not as close to my prayer partners as I normally was. The enemy had come in with dissension among us. One of my closest friends in the group worked in the same beauty salon and we were not on speaking terms.

Initially, I had NO intention of re-marrying my ex-husband Jack. The people had ruled. My Pastor slammed the gavel. I did not go on a fast. I did not really pray about the situation. Once "Pastor" gave the approval the deal was sealed.

After all, Pastor was looking out for my well-being. At the time I had been faithfully under his ministry for ten years. I trusted my Pastor's opinion. I had watched his life over the years and knew his character. He lived what he preached. I had no reason to believe he had any other motives besides reconciling our marriage. He wanted the best for us.

I was confused. I questioned why I went through all that I had gone through concerning my marriage in the first place. Would it be God's will for me to go back to a situation that "I know" He brought me out of so profoundly?

I was in so much pain. I just wanted it to stop by any means necessary. The only way I could describe it, was as though someone literally snatched my heart out of my chest, threw it on the ground, and stomped the very life out of it. These tests were excruciating.

Jack can be very persuasive. He was not letting up. He courted me on the phone. He drove to church "every" Sunday. He took me to dinner as often as he could. He professed his love for me. He told me that there was no one else for him except me. He said I was his soul mate for eternity... blah blah blah.

My feelings for Jack had changed after three years of being completely divorced. I had done the work. I had gone through deliverance. I asked God to take him out of my spirit, and out of my heart. Now he's back asking for my hand in marriage, how crazy is that? What I refer to as "my spiritual equilibrium," was way off. I was barely existing mentally at this point.

Jack was always a lady's man. He promised me things would be different this time. Well, guess what? Two months after Jack's return we walked down the aisle once again in holy matrimony.

Only a few people at church knew that we were going to have a wedding. It was New Year's Eve. A perfect time for celebration. My friends at church all chipped in. My good friend Lona let me use one of her beautiful dresses. Another good friend of mine Vett, brought my bouquet of flowers, and another sister at church taped the wedding music. They were all elated about the wedding.

Nichol was furious that I fell for Dad's old tricks. She could not believe I was going to remarry him after all that he put me through. She did not realize that my judgment was cloudy under stress.

<u>RIP - My Baby Brother Norbert holding Nichol when she was a baby</u>

A Soldier in our US Army

Married Him Twice

Everyone was so excited! We had praise and worship, foot washing, and communion. Pastor made an announcement.

"Surprise! Evangelist Waters is getting remarried tonight!" He announced.

The church went up in an uproar of praise! The choir was singing, and the pastor was praising God. Pastor was so happy as if it was one of his biological daughters getting married. I'm sure he felt he had done his job as a Pastor.

My close friends that attended were in agreement. It was something to behold. My first lady stood as my matron of honor. My brother Rick was Jack's best man. Sammy, Jack's younger sister came to support too. No one else from either side of our families attended. They were not in agreement with our union.

My Mother would have come, but she lived in another state. It all happened so quick. We just went with the flow. I initially asked Nichol to be my maid of honor, she vehemently declined.

"I now pronounce you husband and wife. You may kiss the bride."

Order in the House

Despite the foolishness he carried on in his personal life; Jack was always a disciplinarian as a Dad. Jack raised Nichol since she was four months old. He was actually the only father she knew, since her biological father Skip was murdered when she was six years old.

When we first remarried Nichol was still living at home with me. She went in and out whenever she pleased, continuing the same behavior, for a while anyway. Once Dad reestablished his position as the head of house, he lowered the boom on her. Though we were divorced for three years, he and Nichol had stayed in touch.

When she first decided to live the homosexual lifestyle, she had moved with her father Jack. He was a little more liberal about such issues. Nichol and Jack got along just fine, long as he was out of the will of God. Things were different now that Dad was walking with God again. He was on my side now, so to speak.

At this point and time in Jack's life he wanted some peace. At first, he allowed me to deal with Nichol until he saw how out-of-control she was. He always told me she had me wrapped around her little finger. I will admit, I made exceptions because of her obedience to us. Some may have said she was a little spoiled.

Jack and his family, the Rivers, owned a lucrative tax business in Pasadena, California. Shortly after Jack and I remarried, it was income tax season. Nichol was aware during tax time that Dad was under a lot of pressure. He worked seven days a week, 10 to 12-hour days from January through April. There was no room for any unnecessary drama. This was the only time of the year Jack put demands on me to cook, keep his shirts washed and pressed.

He got in late and went to work early in the morning. A few months into our marriage Jack put his foot down concerning some of the things that Nichol was doing. Though a very quiet man, Jack could always see through muddy water. The jig was up, and Nichol knew it.

She was constantly on her phone talking loud as she came up the driveway. Her lack of discretion annoyed the heck out of her dad. We could hear her a mile away. She brought strangers home all times of night, and would leave them in the den while she showered and dressed for the club.

Jack was a Vietnam Veteran. He did not trust strangers, especially when they were up to no good. He was very suspicious of people that were shady characters. We basically had a stranger living in our home, our daughter Nichol. This certainly was not the little girl we raised.

Jack woke up one night late, and there was a strange man in the den. Jack came to our bedroom to tell me what Nichol was up to. These were people that Nichol would not ordinarily associate with in normal circumstances. Her judgment was not precise, they could have been murderers for all we knew. God protected us so many nights.

She was resentful that I re-married my ex-husband. Now that he was living in the house with us, she could not manipulate my emotions anymore. Dad had come back to save the day. Jack let her know she could no longer bring strange people in our house all hours of the night.

"If you are going to live here you must come home at a decent hour," Jack demanded.

He even issued an ultimatum for her to get a job to support herself.

One thing about the children in the Rivers family, everyone knew that Jack was not one that you would buck up to. He was known for pulling out those "red boxing gloves." If they even looked like they wanted to disrespect him, they were reminded who was the king of the castle.

Jack had a reputation growing up that he could

handle his own. He was not a bully, but he was not a person to be messed with. He also was a minor boxing champion in the United States Marine Corps. He bragged about his boxing record. He took pride in displaying his swift blows to the air as he did the "Mohamed Ali shuffle" in the front yard to keep in shape.

Dad bought Nichol a nice Toyota. Prior to that, Jack and I were chauffeuring her around, unless her friends picked her up. Now she could get around on her own. She had no excuse for not making it to an interview or getting herself a job. She really did not want to work. Nichol just wanted to party all night, and sleep all day.

Nichol played the game for a little while. The crowd that she hung with knew how to work the system. She got a job at a temp agency, which would allow her to work a few days a week, here and there. My husband and I could not believe the behavior she displayed. We certainly did not raise her like that. One thing about Jack was he worked, and was not lazy by any means.

When the jobs at the temp agency ran out, Nichol got a telemarketing job. She did not have any initiative when it came to find a job. She stayed out late clubbing, and then woke up at the last minute trying to get to work on time. She was constantly running late, barely stumbling out the door at the last minute. It was as though we had a child in elementary school all over again.

We had to remind her to get up every morning, rush her out the door, then encourage her not to stay out too late. Mind you, we never had to do any of that when she was coming up in school. Nichol was always so responsible. She made her bed in the mornings before school, kept her room clean, and she always did her homework without being asked. Her new walk of life was the total opposite of her upbringing.

Nichol came home frantic late one night. She was shaking because her back windshield had been shot out. She told us that she was driving through a neighborhood in Watts, California and got caught in a shootout between two cars. The bullet hole in the door panel was an inch wide. I found out later she was affiliated with a gang. I was grateful to God for sparing her life. The next morning, I received a phone call that my co-worker's son was murdered while sitting in his car. I dropped to my knees in gratitude, and cried. That could have very well have been Nichol.

In Los Angeles parking was scarce. Half the battle was getting to work early enough to find a good parking space, and punching that time clock promptly. Nichol began to get parking tickets with addresses all over LA. By the time we found out about them they had gone into penalty with fines included. Unfortunately, the car was in Jack's name. At first, I would pay them trying to make sure she kept that car.

Whenever I thought I had it under control, another ticket came in the mail. Eventually, I had to tell Jack what was going on. He was very upset. We could not keep up with the parking tickets since they were coming so fast. It was apparent to us that Nichol made no effort to read the signs. She parked wherever she wanted to, whenever she got ready. Over a period, Jack paid over $1,000.00 to clear all those tickets.

The cycle went on and on. We paid the tickets off, and she accumulated more. Ultimately, Jack decided to take the car back and park it on the side of the house. Nichol's license got suspended, but that did not stop her from going out. Her life continued to spiral out of control. Her behavior became more erratic.

Nichol went from one job to another trying to appease us. She began to disappear for a few weeks, then come home starting the same cycle over again. To be perfectly honest, we were beginning to feel a relief when she was gone. She was wearing us down. This "new" Nichol had more drama than we were used to dealing with.

Nichol would come home after being on a drug

binge. It was a constant vicious cycle. I worried about Nichol when I did not hear from her. I was uneasy when she was around. I had peace in the house when she was not home. Whew! I just kept praying, fasting, and trusting God.

Nichol got her tongue pierced, and first tattoo. I was shocked when she could barely talk due to the swelling. I kept trying to have a conversation, but she was avoiding me. She was trying to hide the tongue piercing from me. I didn't know what this child was going to come up with next.

Miracle on Meadowbrook

It was pouring down rain, and Nichol came home. It was one of the worst storms we had seen in Los Angeles. She looked worn out.

"Where have you been? I asked, with worry.

"I woke up in Malibu on a bus bench." she said.

"A bus bench," I said, curiously.

"Yeah." she said, as if it was no big deal.

"Why were you on a bus? And why were you in Malibu?" I said.

"I dozed off and it was too late to get a bus going in the opposite direction that late, so I spent the night," Nichol said.

"What is going on?" I asked.

She went on to explain how she got on the bus to come home, which would have been a fifteen minute ride from where she started. She fell asleep, missed her stop, and ended up at the end of the line. She woke up at Malibu beach. She was so high and tired that she laid on the bus bench and fell asleep. When she woke up nothing was missing. She still had her "two" cell phones and a pocket full of money.

My heart dropped. Fear came over me. Nichol was way out of her element. Malibu was not a place that she hung out. The residents of Malibu were rich and famous which we normally saw on TV. Lots of homeless derelicts slept on the beach. That was a very busy high traffic area. Anybody could have saw her on that bus stop kidnapped, robbed or even raped her.

I felt so baffled. I could not understand why she was throwing her life away? This picture made me sad. My poor baby. My only child. How could I reach her? Yet again, GOD, answered my prayer, and brought her home to me. My mind played over and over, what could have happened to her, out on a busy highway, all alone. My God. I sighed with relief, and whispered, "Thank you Jesus."

Nichol was tired and hung-over. Once again, this was my opportunity to get her to lay down and rest. I hid her cell phone, so that her friends couldn't call to get her out the house. She was not making much sense as she began to babble. I don't know what kind of drugs she was taking, but she was very emotional. She needed help getting into the tub.

Once I finally got her over into the water, she began to cry. It was as though she was trying to repent or something. It was all very confusing to me. She took herself under the water.

"In the name of Jesus," she said, before dunking herself backwards.

As she came up out of the water, she began to cry and speak in tongues. My mission was to get her to go to sleep, sober her up so she could come to herself, and stop all this madness.

Then she said to me, with tears streaming down her face. "Mom."

"Yes," I said.

As I washed her back, I was pleading the Blood of Jesus over her.

"Devil let my baby go! In the name of Jesus," I commanded. This was the strangest thing. I did not expect her to say what she said.

"Mom," she said a second time. Still crying.

"What is it?" I calmly said.

"There's this girl, who lives down the street, she's young and she's in a wheelchair Mom," she replied, muffling through tears.

"Somebody needs to pray for her," she cried.

"Who?" I asked.

"You need to pray for her Mom, it's so sad," Nichol cried. "She's young Mom and she's in a wheelchair," she repeated. "Please mom, please call her and pray for her." She pleaded and continued to cry profusely.

I tried to calm her down. I thought maybe she had been high all night on drugs and was just emotional. She would not let it go, she repeated it again. I finally got her out of the bathtub, helped her dry off, and put on her pajamas. Nichol continued to cry.

"I have their phone number Mom. I'm going to call them now and tell them to come down here," Nichol said.

"Okay let's try to reach them after a nap," I said.

I was trying to pacify Nichol because she was so disoriented. Nichol went on to dial the number anyway. I was a nervous wreck and did not know what to do. "Who is she talking about?" I wondered. "Is there really a girl in a wheelchair, or is she delusional from drugs?" However, I went along with the story trying to get her to lay down, but she refused.

I walked around the living room in circles pondering on what my next move would be. The rain was steadily coming down. Moments later the doorbell rang. I went to the door. A tall black man stood on my front porch. I had never seen this young man before. I assumed it was the person Nichol just called.

"Yes, may I help you?" I said.

"Yes ma'am, I'm KJ, I just got a call from Nichol, she told me to bring my wife down, and that you were going to pray for her. She's out in the van in a wheelchair, can you come outside," he said.

I grabbed my umbrella, my blessed oil, and put on my red long coat with a hood on it. It was easier for me to go out to the van than for them to bring her into the house in a wheelchair since it was raining. Out the door I went, not knowing what to expect. I was standing outside of the van talking to this young man, his wife, and his mother-in-law. I introduced myself as Nichol's mother.

It was very awkward. I did not really expect these people to show up in the rain, but they did. It was true, there really was a woman in a wheelchair that needed healing. Since I was talking to strangers, I wanted to explain what was about to take place. I was not sure how much they knew about church or blessed oil.

"Hello," I said.

"Hi," responded the disabled woman in the back.

The sliding door was open on the side of the van.

"Are you all familiar with blessed oil?" I asked.

"Yes ma'am, I'm a backslider. I know all about blessed oil," she said.

"Oh, okay," I said.

My mind immediately shifted into ministry mode. I start encouraging the mother to come back to the Lord. I asked permission if I could anoint her with oil.

The next thing I knew Nichol had come out the house in her pajamas in the rain. I didn't even realize she was behind me. Before I knew it, she reached over me and laid hands on the young lady in the wheelchair. She cried out with authority **"In the name of Jesus! TALITHA CUMI, rise up and walk!"** (which being interpreted means 'Damsel Arise' Mark 5:41)

When Nichol completed her prayer we all stood there for a moment in silence. I was in disbelief. The power of God was undeniably present. The couple and the woman's mother hugged us gratefully. Nichol went back in the house, I followed behind her. I learned something "new" about God that day. He will use "whomever" He wants to use, whenever He gets ready to.

When Nichol moved so swiftly to pray; I was thinking 'What does she think she's doing? God's not going to use her, she's a backslider. I'm the one with clean hands.' All these judgmental thoughts went through my mind. It was evident that the power of God was on her. We serve a mighty, great, and awesome God. He proved to me that day, He is Lord of Lords, and He reigns Supreme.

That experience changed my life in the sense of how I viewed God. Later on, the phone rang.

"Hello," I answered.

There was a man's voice on the other end of the phone.

"Hello it's KJ. I am the husband of the woman you prayed for earlier," he said.

"Yes?" I said.

He wasn't quite sure how to deliver this miraculous testimony.

"My, my, wife, got up out of the wheelchair. She's taking a few steps across the living room. Oh my God! She is walking!" he said.

"What? Wow" I said, surprisingly. "Thank you, Jesus! Thank you, Jesus!" I said, with excitement.

I was shocked. I certainly believed in divine healing, but I was not expecting Nichol to be an instrument. The fact that God used "my daughter," a backslider, to manifest an instantaneous miracle was mind boggling. This increased my faith. There was still hope. Surely, God was going to deliver my baby one day.

If I never learn another thing about God, I learned not to put Him in a box.

Old Family Secret

Nichol was way off emotionally. Her behavior was more bizarre than ever. She was talking a lot, and was not making much sense. She became very angry and irritated over the least little thing. I was glad her dad was home. Her spirit was restless. She moved around unnecessarily. Jack was familiar with the signs of drug use. He sensed that whatever Nichol was high on, it was something more than marijuana or alcohol.

Jack decided he was going pull rank on her. Even though she was an adult, he felt it was best for her to stay home that evening. He told her to go lay down and get some rest. She thought he was joking, and she refused to go to her room. She wanted to leave. She was fidgety, and wanted to get out of that house.

Her dad insisted on her getting some rest. Jack had a way of calming and defusing a situation. He knew Nichol was my heart. He also knew this was a very sensitive time for me. Her behavior made me uneasy. I just wanted her to relax and go to bed. Finally, she got bold.

"I'm leaving, you can't keep me here," Nichol said.

"You are not going anywhere Nichol. Come on in here with us" Jack said, patiently.

Somehow, he got her to come into our bedroom. Once Nichol was on the other side of that door, Jack slowly laid on the floor. He positioned his body across the bedroom door, folded his arms across his chest, and closed his eyes to go to sleep. Nichol was furious.

"What are you doing Dad? Please get up and let me out, I've got to go," she said.

"Nope. You really need to lay down, get some rest," Jack said, peacefully.

Nichol's anger escalated. She began to breathe hard. Then she started crying. She was out-of-control. My heart was beating so fast I didn't know what to do. I was glad Jack was there. Nichol threatened to jump through our glass window if Dad did not move away from the door and let her out.

"If you guys don't let me out of this room, I'm going to tell you something you don't want to hear," she said.

I was lying on my bed very still. Jack was on the floor guarding the door. Nichol was stomping around the room angry. What is she about to say? My heart was racing. Nichol again made an attempt to convince Dad to let her out of our room. Jack did not budge. Nichol started crying again.

"I was molested by someone when I was young."

I sat up in the bed.

"Who was it," I said.

"It was Larry," she said.

It was so quiet in the room you could hear a mouse licking on ice. I exhaled. Larry was one Jack's sons from a previous marriage. Though I was upset, I was relieved. What I suspected all along finally had come out. Years prior, I used to have dreams of a silhouette of a man standing in the doorway of Nichol's room. In the dream she was a young girl. I had that dream on several occasions.

I asked Nichol as a child if anyone had ever tried to touch her in a sexual way. She responded the same whenever I confronted her. The answer was 'no.' Now that Nichol revealed the details of what happened long ago, she agreed to stay in for the night. You could feel a load lift off her. She climbed in the bed with me and went to sleep. Jack remained on the floor guarding the door until morning. We all got a good night's rest.

I advised Jack not to mention it to Larry's mother, or any of the family members until we got all the facts. I wanted to pray and get direction from God on how we should handle the situation. I was grateful that God did not allow me to gain knowledge of this until I was rooted and grounded in the Lord. I can truly say if I had known it any sooner, I might be proclaiming the Gospel from inside prison walls...yep, a prison ministry for sure.

Jack felt as her father that he should do something. He handled it in the only way he felt was right. He confronted Larry face to face. He also called Larry's mother to inform her.

I called my pastor's wife to seek help for Nichol, and hopefully receive counsel. The next day I drove Nichol to the pastor's house. She spent the day with the first lady who had mentored her coming up. It seemed Nichol had a sense of comfort after going over there.

Nichol was conflicted. Her day of vindication was finally here. I can't imagine what that must have been like for her to keep such a secret for all those years. My poor baby. I felt so guilty for having married into such a crazy family. There were so many dynamics to the Rivers family.

Sometimes in life we make decisions that have consequences, and those choices cost us a significant price.

Once the word was out in the Rivers family that Larry was possibly a molester, the phone calls began to come in. It was a mess. My husband's ex-wife, Joan, would not believe her son could do such a thing. Jack's outspoken mother, Joyce, who was "the voice of influence" in the family, called with her opinion. When Joyce asked to speak to Nichol, she refused to talk with her. Joyce was always trying to resolve the lives of her children and grandchildren whether they wanted to hear it or not.

The phone was ringing off the hook. Jack's sisters were calling and his dad. I was determined to protect Nichol. We eventually had silence the ringer. I called my mother and members of my side of the family. At the time I only called the family members that were going to be positive and pray instead of fight.

One of my step-sons, Greg, who Jack had fathered with his first wife Nanette, was leaning towards believing Nichol. He told me a story about an incident when he came to live with us for a year when they were in their teens. He said that Larry used to put tacks in Nichol's bed for a prank. I got upset immediately after hearing that. I could not imagine how a teenager cold be so cruel to my innocent baby.

Greg was quite different from Larry. Reflecting back, he agreed that it was likely Larry was guilty of sexual abuse. Greg and Larry were the same age, born two weeks apart; by two different women. Greg knew Larry had issues, and was a little afraid of his brother. It appeared to me when they were coming up, Larry was more aggressive than Greg.

At first Jack believed Nichol, but later, after hearing his son Larry's side, he began to question if he made the right choice. Jack was under a tremendous amount of pressure from both sides of the family. I reminded him of when we were married the first time, how I woke up one night to Nichol's cry. I ran upstairs to see what was wrong. Nichol was about three or four years old. When I ask her what was wrong, she said, crying, "Something is sticking me." This happened more than once, but I never did find any tacks. My motherly instincts kicked in. I hesitantly confronted Jack and asked a question I was uncomfortable to ask.

"Do you think Larry would harm Nichol?" I said.

Jack blew up!

"No! Larry would never do anything to harm Nichol. He loves Nichol" Jack said, angrily.

He made me feel so bad.

"How could you accuse Larry of such a thing." he went on to say.

I was fearful and speechless.

I remember another incident a few years after the complaints of something sticking her as a child while sleep. I discovered discharge in Nichol's cartoon underwear. That

97

certainly was not normal for a 6 year old. I drilled her persistently. Nichol insisted that she hit her private on the middle bar of her bike. I took her to the doctor, and I was told that her hymen was not broken.

Jack had a bad temper, and could at times, be very intimidating. Almost anything could set him off, especially if things were not going his way. I was not going to let it go. When it came to my baby, I was very protective. I kept a close watch after that.

Larry was a very deceitful teen. He was thirteen when I met him. We were just ten years apart in age. He was intelligent, but he did not fit the mode of what society called a "normal" teenage boy. He did not party when he was young. He was more of a homebody. He often brought home a stray dog asking if he could keep it. Larry was the type you may catch burning a lizard in the back yard. Though he was a handsome young guy, there was always something a little unsettling about him.

Larry had some resentment towards me. His father made the decision to leave his mom in pursuit of me. I believe Larry never forgave his dad for leaving his mother. Once Jack divorced Larry's mom, I don't believe Larry ever got over it. Jack's choices affected him greatly. Sons are very protective of their mothers. The same week that Jack and I got married, Larry's mother Joan sent him to live with us.

His loyalty to his mother always caused him to put up a wall between the two of us. Sometimes we would be having a good time, and right in the middle of laughter he would shut down emotionally. I believe the pressure of having to stay loyal to his Mom ate away at him.

I may be wrong in my theory, though I don't think I am. I assume because Larry was so young when his parents split up he became very vengeful. He took that frustration out on my baby to pay me back for being what he felt was a home wrecker. Looking back in hindsight, it was all very dysfunctional. I am by no means making excuses for Larry, he was in his teens, and knew right from wrong.

Unfortunately, Nichol in her innocence, became the victim. Another life ruined. Not only was she robbed of her innocence, but her childhood as well. All this happened to my child right under my roof. Nichol was hurt when she discovered that Dad did not believe her. The look on her face, as tears streamed down her cheeks, broke my heart. I knew she was being truthful. Nichol was never known to be dishonest. My believing her was more of a confirmation of my spiritual instinct than anything else since there was no concrete evidence of her childhood recollection.

"Dad doesn't believe me Mom," Nichol said. She was fragile after her secret of the molestation was exposed. Exhausted from life, it all was taking a toll on her.

Out the Nest

Nichol was too wild for us, so we gave her a deadline to move. Jack made it clear that if she did not change her lifestyle, by no means would she use 'us' as a crutch any longer. It was time for her to grow up. She began to look for an apartment.

I knew she was not emotionally prepared to go out in the world. I had to allow her space to become independent. Los Angeles is a very expensive place to live. At first, the only affordable places that she found were in the shady parts of the city.

I prayed and asked God to please allow her to find a nice safe place to live. I knew Nichol was not living the life that would allow her to receive the blessings of the Lord. I would not be able to sleep at night imagining someone breaking into her house. This would be the first time that Nichol and I had lived apart.

I don't think I would have been so concerned if she had not been as fragile and broken from her life choice. What she was doing was not who she was. I believe had she been the kind of daughter who was fast, sassy, or rebellious, it would have been easier for me to kick her out. Sometimes, young people need tough love, but this was not the case. Nichol felt violated and wanted revenge. She wanted to be vindicated and to be heard. As a result, Nichol became very bitter.

One day, Nichol and I were out having lunch at one of our favorite Mexican restaurants. She found a particular apartment that she really liked, and decided to look no further. The manager had given her the owner's phone number, since he was not sure about renting to someone under twenty-five. She already had shown me the place, it was beautiful. I was happy that it was ten minutes away from me.

For some reason the owner was trying to put her in one of his properties over on the east side of town, which was rough. The building in that part of town was not quite as nice. I heard the voice of the Lord say to me, 'Pray with her and believe me; and after you pray tell Nichol to call the owner back and the apartment is hers.' I told Nichol what the Lord said. I took her hand in the restaurant and began to pray. "Lord for thy servant's sake, I'm asking you to give my daughter this apartment. I know she's not living right, but please do this for me Lord, and I will forever give you praise in Jesus name," I said.

The power of God was in that prayer and God's presence was right at our table. Nichol immediately called the owner. She asked him if he had made the decision to rent the apartment to her.

The owner said, "Yes!"

We rejoiced in that restaurant that day. I told the Lord "Thank you." Once again, He answered my prayer.

I was thinking maybe this might cause her to mature. I was hoping Nichol would get in her own place, get a good job, snap out of it, get herself together, and come back to the Lord. She knew that God definitely made a way for her. I thought, 'Surely she is going to acknowledge His favor and grace.'

Nichol got a few of her new worldly friends to help her move. Jack and I agreed to let her take her bed and the furniture that was in her room. Away she went to Mc Clung Drive. I was relieved, the apartment was nice, and there was a security gate downstairs. Nichol lived upstairs, and I was glad about that. Maybe now I could get some rest, but it was not so.

Nichol took it to yet another level. This new-found freedom allowed her to do what she wanted, whenever she wanted to. She took on a new name, "Esko" with the motto "the Party Monster." Her place became the hangout. It was centrally located right in the heart of Los Angeles, in an urban community called Leimert Park.

The view from her living room window was of a well known street called Crenshaw, which was nicknamed "the Shaw." That's where the low-riders gathered on Sunday afternoon to show off their cars. There was a huge mall right across the street from her called the Crenshaw-Baldwin Mall. The well-kept community was surrounded by Black owned businesses. Soul food restaurants, Jamaican food, and some of the best burger stands in town were in the area. There were nail salons, beauty salons and barber shops, which were all black owned. All of these establishments were all up and down Crenshaw.

Nichol had moved right in the middle of the action. People set up booths to sale baskets on holidays. On one corner the Black Muslims sold bean pies. You might see someone with a Bible and a sign that read "Jesus Saves." Crenshaw was live, and 'in living color.'

Nichol again was exposed to another world in itself. Sometimes, when I went over there I could not get into the building. This brought on another form of worry. I had prayed for her to get the apartment, God answered that prayer. I had prayed for it to be secure, God honored that prayer. Now, I did not have access to the building. There was no buzzer downstairs, I would have to call Nichol to get inside. Most the time she would not answer her phone.

I recall one occasion I went to Nichol's apartment and as usual I could not get in. It was hard to find parking, so I had to park three blocks away. The enemy played tricks on my mind. I was in fear that she was up there in some type of danger. When she did not answer her phone, I went around the back.

I looked up at her window to see if there was any light in her room. I saw a ray of something. I began to call her name. She never answered. I drove around the neighborhood to see if her car was parked anywhere. I saw her car a few blocks away. I sat in my car and prayed. I tried to cast down thoughts of worry and anxiety, but my feelings overpowered me. Sometimes two days passed before I could reach her.

Gremlins Attack

One Sunday, Jack suggested we take Nichol to dinner. We called to let her know we were coming. She let us in the gate. When we walked into her apartment, there were people asleep on the floor. There was cocaine on a plate sitting on the table. Also, I noticed small piles of marijuana laying around. Nichol was so glad to see us. She left her guests to go with us and eat.

The unruly house guests had been there for weeks. There was a gay man and a transsexual, which is someone who is biologically born a man with breast implants. These two, had set up a home office right inside my daughter's apartment. There were computers plugged in, an extra phone jack was installed, and they were altering receipts for a same day cash return on merchandise.

"What's going on at your house Nichol?" Jack asked.

"These people I know came in town for a ball and got stranded because they ran out of money," she replied.

They came to visit California. Their scam, writing bad checks on Rodeo' Drive in Beverly Hills went sour. Through this conversation we learned Nichol had been recruited into a gay sorority called "Houses." She explained to us that someone was flying her all over the US to compete in a type of pageant called "balls." Her Dad and I never heard of such.

The Bible describes the characteristics of those who choose to live a gay lifestyle in Romans 1:26-32 (NLT). It says, *"That is why God abandoned them to their shameful desires. Even the women turned against the natural way to have sex and instead indulged in sex with each other. And the men, instead of having normal sexual relations with women, burned with lust for each other. Men did shameful* *things with other men, and as a result of this sin, they suffered within themselves the penalty they deserved. Since they thought it foolish to acknowledge God, he abandoned them to their foolish thinking and let them do things that should never be done. Their lives became full of every kind of wickedness, sin, greed, hate, envy, murder, quarreling, deception, malicious behavior, and gossip. They are backstabbers, haters of God, insolent, proud, and boastful. <u>They invent new ways of sinning, and they disobey their parents.</u> They refuse to understand, break their promises, are heartless, and have no mercy. They know God's justice requires that those who do these things deserve to die, yet they do them anyway. Worse yet, they encourage others to do them, too."*

This passage of scripture made the outlook of this lifestyle very plain to me from God's perspective. It was clear that there was no future in this charade. What was Nichol going to come up with next? She had a bag full of surprises. The saga went on and on. It was all an illusion. She was flying out of town, getting new clothes, coming home sleeping for days, and partying all night.

Daily she had the same routine. We later found out Nichol was selling drugs. I wondered how she supported herself because we stopped funding her party a long time ago. I was disappointed in her actions, but she was still my child. I had to keep a positive mindset without giving in, or accepting her lifestyle.

I know that Satan comes to bring division, so I made sure to keep the lines of communication open.

Good Intentions

Nichol was mentally exhausted during the three months her guests overstayed their welcome. The gay lifestyle was taking a toll on her emotionally. She realized that her associations were leeches. They ate up all her food, hitched rides, and slept at her house when they came in town for "the balls" (gay sorority pageants).

She called me one day when her car was broken down in front of her house. She had partied away her money. Her car was parked on the wrong side of the street due to street sweeping scheduled.

"Where are all your friends?" I asked.

"Everybody left," she replied, sadly.

Some years passed since Nichol had been out there. I was going on with my life, realizing she had made her choice. At times, my emotions got the best of me. I continued to pray and fast believing God for her deliverance.

I was over at a church member's house one evening when Nichol called. I sensed she was coming to her wits end. She asked me if I could have her car towed. She sounded discouraged. I gave her friends the nickname "Gremlins."

Another day Nichol showed up at our house, pulled her car up in the driveway, and covered it up. She stayed at our house for weeks, which turned into months. Nichol was on the verge of a nervous breakdown. She ate, slept, and only came out of her room for short periods of times. She was drained and depleted. Nichol turned off her cell phone. She told one close friend to spread the word that she was done.

Jesus is the Source

"Return, ye backsliding children, and I will heal your backslidings." Jeremiah 3:22a (KJV)

My heart went out to Nichol watching her pitiful disposition. Spiritually, she relinquished all rights when she went down in that watery grave of baptism in the name of Jesus. She carried a gift that was "priceless" on the inside of her, the Holy Spirit. It was as though she regretted making the decision to give her life to Christ at eight years old. God did not make a mistake saving her at such a young age. I prayed that she would make the right choice.

The Devil did not want to let my baby go. I saw the anguish on her face. Nichol was indecisive, miserable, and tormented. Her back was against the wall. Seven years of her life had passed by. She had dropped out of college. Her only work experience was limited. The only jobs she had were through temporary employment agencies. She chose to party and hang out with gang bangers instead of going to college to secure her future.

Nichol invested a lot of time in a life that was all an illusion. The Devil had sucked the life out of her; recruiting her to be showcased in a gay sorority called Houses. I could see with my spiritual eyes a bunch of demons devouring my child. She was blinded by the glamour. She had become popular and all the attention overwhelmed her.

For all that is in the world, the lust of the flesh, and the lust of the eyes, and the pride of life, is not of the Father, but is of the world. 1 John 2:16 (KJV)

However, Jack and I still nursed her back to some sort of sanity. Our lives were put on hold once again to cater to her. All the years Jack and I had been together we never lived alone. Jack had three children by two different

108

marriages, and at some time or another they either lived with us or were visiting with us. On occasion I had family members that lived with us too. There was always someone living at, what I referred to as the "Shady Rest Hotel."

When Jack and I remarried the children were grown, but Nichol was considered the baby of the family. We knew she had great potential, so we were trying to work through these difficult years in her life. I am sure Nichol did not realize the access she had given to the demonic realm. Once she entertained one spirit, then several others invaded into her life causing a tailspin of confusion, deception, and hopelessness.

There she was, with nothing to show for the past seven years. We know from experience it's never too late to get yourself together. We tried to encourage her to take some sort of job training class, and pull herself up out of this dark hole.

Nichol bagged up all her men's wardrobe to give away. Some items she discarded into the garbage. She was making a huge step to conquer this journey. The pressure of the separation anxiety put a tremendous weight upon her. In spite of all that, I thought she was making great progress.

Once Nichol began to gain her strength she allowed her hair to grow back, and slowly started transitioning back into women's attire. I was ecstatic! She was coming back to church. All my prayers have been answered. It was difficult for her to go back to church after being gone so long. I could tell she was uncomfortable in the women's clothes. It was awkward for her at first. I thought if she let her hair grow back she would be right back to her old self again. I got my friend's daughter to braid her hair in extensions until it was long enough for me to arrange her hair in a style.

On a Monday night prayer, Nichol repented down at the altar. She started witnessing to some of the people that she knew from the streets. They came to church, the Lord saved them, and their kids. Things were going well. A total of six adults and two children were baptized in Jesus name and filled with the Holy Ghost.

Shortly after Nichol got restored, the first lady of our church suddenly passed away of a heart attack. It was on Mother's Day morning. Nichol had only been back to church for a short period of time when this happened. This was the first Mother's Day in years that I was going to church with my daughter.

I will never forget that day. Jack was out in the front yard watering the grass. He had no plans on coming to church because he was now backslidden. Jack traditionally always cooked Mother's Day brunch for all the mothers in our family.

I was planning to enjoy my day. Jack's absence at church was not going to ruin it. I had my hair curled just right, had on my beautiful red suit, and my pearl necklace. Nichol was also beautifully dressed.

The day was absolutely gorgeous. The sun was shining so bright, the sky was clear. We had the front door open and Jack was playing some jazz on the front porch. The phone rang, and it was my good friend Lona. I answered upbeat and excited!

"Praise the Lord!" I said, bubbly.

"You don't know, do you?" she asked, in a serious tone.

"Know what?" I asked, as my heart pounded.

"Sister Crocker died," she said, in a voice full of sorrow.

I lost my breath, I could not breathe. I fell to my knees screaming as I pulled on my pearl necklace. I was sobbing uncontrollably. Nichol stood looking at me puzzled.

"What happened Mom?" she asked.

Through the tears, I could hardly catch my breath.

"Sister Crocker died! This is Auntie Lona," I cried out.

Nichol took the phone to complete the call. Jack heard the screams from the front yard, and ran in to see what all the commotion was about. Mother's Day was ruined. I really took her death hard. Nichol was speechless.

The devastation of losing our First Lady took a toll on all of us. Nichol was very discouraged after her death. She had a close relationship with Sister Crocker as a young girl through her teens. There was a time in her life she was like another mother to Nichol. I believe Nichol regretted the fact that she never allowed herself to get that close to her again. Nichol had remained very guarded around her after she returned to church.

Our Pastor remarried two months later. Nichol was not in agreement with this decision. She felt like he totally disregarded the first lady's memory. One of her newly saved friends also felt it was too soon, so she left the church and never returned. I know there was no sin in Pastor's decision, but it affected several people in different ways.

Nichol began to associate with old acquaintances, which were the lesbian women that just got saved. She figured since all of them were in church now they could fellowship together. Nichol was not strong enough to interact with them on a regular basis. As we know evil communication corrupts good manner (1 Corinthians 15:33 KJV). Nichol struggled with her Christian walk. After about seven months, Nichol left the church again. The other friends left the church too.

Warning Comes

Warning comes before destruction (Hebrews 2:1 KJV).

God had given Nichol a dream about a big black snake under her kitchen sink. The snake was coiled up looking at her as though it was waiting to strike. I knew it was a warning from God not to leave from under His umbrella of safety. Since she did not go through any deliverance such as: fasting and renunciations, she began to build the things she once destroyed (Galatians 2:18 KJV).

Nichol did not take heed to the warning, and fled back into her sinful lifestyle. Reflecting back, I believe she came back to church because she wanted to make us proud of her at the time, and was looking for a temporary relief from her troubled situation. She was not ready to submit and fully commit to her calling. I was hoping for the best, but again she let me down.

Not long after she left the church, the enemy sent a woman who was on an assignment to finish Nichol off. She was the big black snake that God had warned Nichol about in the dream. My daughter chopped her hair right back off to get into character. I was so upset that she decided to cut her hair after all the work we put into growing it out. I felt like it would have saved me some embarrassment if she looked like a woman. The Lord checked me.

"It's not about her hair. It is about her heart," the Holy Spirit spoke to me.

That was the deception of the enemy making me think I could do less explaining if her appearance was not so extreme. God knew what she was doing, and I had to swallow my pride. I was so caught up in the opinions of others and God knew it all anyway.

I was led to leave my job and go into full time

ministry. A year later, Jack and I separated. Eventually, we divorced for the final and last time. I no longer could afford to live in my house. I ended up moving into Nichol's apartment. She on the other hand moved in with an older woman named Candy. This woman began to replace Nichol's men's wardrobe all over again.

Jack moved back to Pasadena. I lost everything. Some sisters from my church helped move my belongings to Nichol's apartment. I did the only thing I knew to do, which was turn to the Lord in prayer. I thought the testing of my faith, toiling over Nichol was behind me. I girded up realizing that this warfare was going into part two. When a person backslides, things get worse than they were in the beginning. I ended up living in Nichol's place for about seven years.

Nichol would stop by the house to check her mail and leave. I became curious wondering who this person was that she was living with. I told her I wanted to meet this woman. One day, she came by the house to introduce me to Candy. She was only ten years younger than me.

Nichol's girlfriend Candy told me a dramatic story that had us both in tears. She was raped as a teenager by a several men, and had a baby as a result of this travesty. I immediately went into ministry mode, and began to tell her about Jesus. Before she left the house, I asked her if I could pray for her, and she agreed. I laid hands on her, the power of God knocked her out on the floor. I also prayed for Nichol. God demonstrated His power once again.

The relationship between Nichol and this woman was very chaotic. I received phone calls in the middle of the night from Nichol asking me to pick her up. She would be in tears, but she would always go back the next day. I was in constant prayer for her safety. I was afraid that this crazy woman was going to kill my daughter.

I went up into the nightclub to get Nichol one night. A good church friend named Anna went "Behind Enemy

113

Lines" with me. As we approached the venue we could see the demons manifesting in people passing by us. Nichol had been living at Candy's house, and I had not heard from her in weeks. I decided Nichol was going home with me this night. I was tired of this older lady manipulating my daughter, and isolating her away from family. Fortunately, Candy was on the dance floor when we found Nichol inside the club. I kidnapped my own grown daughter. We went back to Anna's house and had a slumber party. My friend Anna was always so hospitable and never judged Nichol, but exhibited the love of God.

I was trying to convince Nichol to stay at her own apartment with me. I had a bad feeling about her dealing with this older woman. I thought I could somehow protect her. The domestic violence occurred so often that I thought someone might end up really injured.

Sometimes when the two of them got into a fight, the woman would throw Nichol's clothes outside in front of her apartment. Candy was an immature attention seeker. Another time Nichol called me for a ride. I picked her up and her white t-shirt was filthy. Oil stains were all over it from hiding under a car. Candy was driving around looking for her. Nichol was out of breath and afraid. As I drove up the street where she told me to meet her, she ran out of nowhere, and jumped in my car.

I woke up in the middle of a warm summer night. I heard a woman screaming. I looked out the window at a car parked across the street up on the grass. A lady was being beaten by someone. I thought it was Nichol being assaulted by that crazy girlfriend Candy. I ran downstairs in my robe and pajamas, jumped on hood of car, and realized after looking in the window it was not Nichol. I was so embarrassed. It was a woman getting beat up by a man. At least my heroic action stopped the man from attacking her further that night.

I was determined that the enemy was going to loose

his grips on my daughter. Every time Nichol came by the house I anointed her with oil. I went to Candy's house several times to get Nichol's belongings. She would come home for a few days, but she kept going back.

Years passed, Nichol wanted to leave her girlfriend Candy. She was gripped with fear. She called me constantly asking for prayer. Once on my way to a retreat with my church I stopped by their house. I demanded her to get her things while the woman was not home. Nichol was scared to leave. She was tormented. I reminded her who she was in God.

"Mom the only way she's going to let me go is if she's dead. Please pray that God kills her, so that I can get out of here," Nichol said, serious.

"I'm not going to say that prayer, you have the Holy Ghost, so use your power," I said.

I left and went on to the women's retreat.

Tough Times

While at the women's retreat my niece, Tanesha called. She was at college in Augusta, Georgia at the time, which was two hours away from my mother's house. Tanesha could hardly talk.

"Grandma has been diagnosed with Stage 4 Cancer Auntie," she said, crying.

"Calm down baby we are going to believe God for a miracle! I'm not receiving that report," I said.

Some sisters circled around me and we began to pray.

The next day I returned home from the retreat and booked my flight to head to Atlanta. I was strengthened for the journey ahead after fellowshipping with the women of God all weekend. I dropped my luggage off at Mama's house, and went to the hospital. I had my prayer shawl and my oil. I anointed Mama and placed that prayer shawl across her body.

"Your siblings got two days to get to Georgia, so call and let them know," the Holy Spirit said to me.

I relayed the message to them, and they planned to get there. I called Nichol to notify her too.

"Nichol, Grandma is not going to live much longer," I said.

"What! Oh no! where is she? I want to hear her voice," Nichol said, tearing up.

"Hold on I will let you speak to her," I said, passing the phone.

"Grandma I love you! I know you are a pillar of prayer. I thank you for being such a loving Grandma," Nichol said.

"I love you sweet pea. Be good baby. Jesus loves you," Mama said, in a low tone.

The next morning the doctors came in to discuss Mama's fate with us. When everyone exited it was just me

116

and Mama. She glanced out the window toward the heavens. "It's between me and Jesus now baby," Mama said, as one tear rolled down her left cheek.

I was speechless as I held her hand.

"This is the ultimate healing," the Holy Spirit spoke softly to me.

I got excited.

"Mama you are going to beat me out of here. You are going to see Jesus!" I said.

We stared at each other with a smile.

Mama wanted to go home and pass away there. Hospice care delivered a bed to her house. I had the atmosphere permeating with worship music. I kept gospel music playing a DVD of my pastor preaching on the TV. Everyone who came to say their last good byes was sad. Many were shocked that she was diagnosed, and dying so soon thereafter.

That Sunday morning, before Mama died, her pastor, first lady, and the saints came by on their way to church. Two people were filled with the Holy Ghost in the living room. I was slinging oil, and proclaiming the gospel to lost souls. The power of God fell on them, and they were speaking in tongues. Mama was in the back with members from her church singing old hymns around her bed. At 10 PM that Sunday night she took her last breath.

Nichol was entangled with that controlling woman Candy. She was conflicted with the idea of coming to her grandmother's service. Candy was so clingy that Nichol knew it would be like pulling teeth to break away from her. On the other hand, she did not want to embarrass me showing up at her grandmother's homegoing dressed as a man.

Rest in Paradise Mama 2 Thessalonians 4:13-18

Concerning them which are asleep, that ye sorrow not, even as others which have no hope.

One month later, my brother Ricky was in the last stages of his life battling Cancer. He had been ill for years, so I knew he was going to be expiring soon. I believed God for his healing, but things looked pretty dim. He lived in Moreno Valley, Ca. almost two hours outside of Los Angeles. I had been spending time with him on a regular basis for the past year.

I took him to his last doctor's appointment. They wanted to try a new procedure, but Ricky was tired. After flying back from burying Mama and tying up some business affairs there; I called my brother Ricky.

"Sis I'm trying to wait on you. Why aren't you here? Ricky asked.

"The plane is landing now brother I am driving straight there," I replied.

I called Nichol to see if she would ride with me. I should have known Candy was not letting Nichol out of her sight. Candy volunteered to drive her out to his house. Ricky was given the same scenario as Mama. Once the Doctor determined there was nothing else that could be done, he was given two days to live after they took him off the medicine. Ricky wanted to go to his own house to die. They delivered a hospital bed in the living room.

Nichol and Candy got there, and Ricky was going in and out of sedation. As he was laying there incoherent Nichol held his hand. Candy had never met any of our family besides me. Candy was standing at my dying brother's bedside. Something rose up in me.

"Candy, you need to have a seat. You don't know my brother, so give Nichol some space," I said, boldly.

I was appalled that this woman would not have any common sense to stay in the background. Candy did not say a word, but politely took a seat.

Ricky passed the next day. Nichol came to the funeral without Candy. She honored one of her favorite uncle's memory, and wore women's clothes. I got her a wig and a

119

nice women's pantsuit. It was a beautiful homegoing service. I said goodbye to my brother and friend. I was deeply saddened, but God knows what's best. My brother was no longer suffering, he was saved, and I knew I would see him again one day in paradise. Relying on God's strength, I pressed forward trusting in God to see me through.

Ricky is in a better place! *To be absent from the body is to be present with the Lord (2 Cor. 5:8)*

I was divorcing Jack for the second time. I had to be in court in two weeks to finalize the divorce. I was going through so much. Jack end up swindling me out of over $200,000 of my retirement. When his mother passed away he placed the money he inherited from her estate in an annuity account.

Jack assured me that the money we spent in our savings would be replaced by the money in the annuity account for our retirement. I was not aware that in the state of California a spouse had no legal rights to inheritance funds in a divorce settlement. The judge said I needed a written statement signed by my ex-husband that the funds were for our retirement, otherwise I had no proof the money belonged to me. I was in shock.

Through it all God kept me.

I continued to pray for Nichol's deliverance. I literally called prayer warriors from all over the United States to intercede for Nichol. The enemy turns the heat up when he knows he's at the end of his road. One thing I can say, dealing with Nichol kept me fervent in prayer and fasting. I was crying out to God one day on her behalf. In the midst of my tears I heard a voice. The Lord spoke to me just as clear. It was a sharp rebuke.

"If I wanted to take her very breath out of her nostrils while she was laying in your lap there is nothing you could do. I don't know why you are falling out. You did not shed a drop of blood for her, and I love her more than you ever could," the Holy Spirit said to me.

The Lord was reminding me He was sustaining Nichol, not me. I repented. God had covered Nichol all this time through all sorts of situations, and I had the nerve to be tired. He brought her too far to leave her now.

After going through many crazy incidents with Candy, Nichol was finally fed up with her shenanigans. The straw that broke the camel's back was when Candy had found Nichol a job, forged work history, and used both of her cell phone numbers to verify the information as a previous employer. She was determined to make Nichol bring in extra income while she was on a medical leave.

After the ninety-day probationary period was passed Nichol got some mail about her health and dental insurance. Unbeknownst to her, Candy had made herself the beneficiary on a $60,000 life insurance policy. Nichol was in disbelief, and never confronted Candy about it. Nichol never applied for a policy because I already carried one on her since childhood.

She canceled the policy, but had to have a friend sign off as a witness. Nichol maneuvered away from Candy permanently. That situation opened Nichol's eyes to see this woman was capable of murder. I exhaled a sigh of relief after seven years of bondage my daughter was out of that unhealthy relationship.

I recall after their break-up going to run some errands. Mysteriously both of my tires on the driver's side were flat. My brother came by with a portable air pump. I discovered that the air was let out my tires. Nichol believed Candy was responsible for this sick joke. That was her way of letting Nichol know she was bitter. The break-up was real this time. Candy got the hint after a few months, and stopped lurking around. Oddly, she moved one street over with the exact same address as ours, but never bothered Nichol.

The number of completion is seven, and that vile relationship had run its course. Nichol made up her mind to get free from Candy. She moved back to Mc Clung Drive to her own apartment. When I tell you, God is so merciful he answered my prayers repeatedly. I was rejoicing. I believed that this was it, she is done, it's over!

I had an internal discussion, 'Surely, Nichol's coming back to church for good. What is it going to take?' I was wrong in my assumption. Nichol was so glad to get free from that demon possessed woman. Now, she wanted to be independent and sow her wild oats, as they say. She still had a few more flames to light up.

I was so stressed out worrying about Nichol to the point my hair was coming out. I was toiling in my sleep one night. The Lord woke me up, and I sat straight up in my bed. A popular lawyer's commercial was on the screen.

"Go to sleep I will fight for you!" the man said, pointing at the TV camera.

"I am fighting for you get some rest," the Holy Spirit whispered.

God used that commercial to give me peace. I laid down and went back to sleep.

The enemy is on an assignment to conjure up ways to cause us to fall. He is an accuser of the brethren. The Lord revealed to me that the attack on Nichol was designed to target the anointing that was on my life. Since the Devil could not get to me he went after my seed.

Demonic forces attempt to wear us down by any means necessary.

After many years of warfare, I began to feel restless and anxious about my future. When you give out so much of yourself, sometimes you need to see the fruit of our labor. I remember wondering if my life would ever be normal? There were questions I entertained, if whether or not I would ever see my daughter become married, or would I be alive to see her deliverance?

Slipped a Mickey

I kept believing that God would deliver Nichol, but had no clue "when" it was going to manifest. I was in a season of limbo. That place in our life when it seems as though God is not answering. I was feeling a bit frustrated.

My faith was my spiritual currency.

The enemy seized the moment. The Devil is patient, and has no problem waiting for the opportunity to create havoc. He preyed on my vulnerability, and without hesitation he swooped in for the kill. In this unbalanced state, I was open to temptation.

I was in a strange place spiritually in my walk with God. I was sitting in Nichol's living room meditating. I remember feeling defeated as I began to assess my life. I had suffered so much loss, yet God continued to strengthen me. By society's standard, I would have been considered to be unsuccessful. My marriage had failed twice, lost my court settlement, my funds were scarce, and my daughter was living every way but right. My good friend Lona called me.

"Hello," I answered.

"Praise the Lord! I'm going up North to a council meeting, why don't you come go with me?" she said,

Lona and I had been traveling buddies for years, and attended many church events together. However, I was not in the mood to take this trip.

"I don't think so. I'm just not up for the ride. I'll pray about it and get back with you," I said, hesitantly.

"Oh, come on and go girl, you need to get away. It will be good for you," she said.

After seeking the Lord in prayer, I decided to take the trip with Lona. The day before we departed she suggested that I contact an old friend of ours name Minister Chuck. He

125

lived in the city where the meeting was being held. I had not seen the young man in about ten years. Ironically, Lona's daughter contacted me the same day.

"Hi Sister Yevette, Brother Chuck messaged me on Facebook, and asked me for your phone number. I gave it to him, I did not think you'd mind," she said, excitedly.

"Oh no! I can't believe you did that," I said, chuckling.

I knew she did not think it was a problem, since he was saved, and we all knew him well. Personally, I didn't give out anyone's phone number without their permission. I met Chuck about ten years prior through Nichol. She had met him at a summer convention in Indianapolis her senior year of high school. Though I had no issues with the young man, I was not comfortable with my number being given to him.

Minister Chuck had expressed to me when he was younger that he had a crush on me. I never thought about dating a younger guy. Besides that, he was about sixteen years under me. At the time I had considered it to be a boyish infatuation, though the sentiments were flattering. I was mature enough to know better. I was not going to allow my integrity to be compromised. Over the years we developed a close spiritual bond, and I became more of a mentor to him. Later he got married and started a family, while I remarried my ex-husband. We eventually lost contact until now.

My friend and I went to the church council. The trip was just what the doctor ordered. We had a great ride up to Northern California. I was so glad I went. When we arrived at the church Chuck was there. It was wonderful to see him again after all those years.

After church was over Chuck and I went out for late dinner. We laughed and talked and shared what our lives had been like over the past ten years. All the problems I was having seemed to disappear. His company was a breath of fresh air.

"It's so good to see you Yevette," Chuck said.

"It's good to see you as well," I replied.

"How long are you all going to be here?" Chuck said.

"Just a few days," I said.

"Maybe we can spend more time together before you leave the city," Chuck said.

"Sounds great!" I said, happily.

While catching up on our lives we discovered that we both had been divorced since we had last seen each other.

The next night there was a ninetieth birthday dinner held for the Bishop of the church at a really nice hall. My friend Lona and I went. Chuck came with his father. The dinner was very festive. They had a red carpet set up in the lobby to take pictures, and my church hosted the dinner in their beautiful matching colors and corsages.

There was chemistry between Chuck and I. We had a great time laughing and getting reacquainted. Chuck had grown up quite a bit. He had earned his Master's Degree, had a great job, and owned his own condo. He was a tall handsome guy with a smile that lit up a room. If only he was a little older. I was leaving the next day and we decided to go out before I left. My girlfriend Lona and I drove back to Los Angeles shortly after saying goodbye.

Now that Nichol was out of the will of God; the Devil conjured up a weapon to try to blindside me. Chuck started to call me periodically. One conversation in particular Chuck decided to pursue me.

"Hey Yevette, you know I still find you very attractive right?" Chuck said.

"Oh really?" I said, surprised.

"Yes, how do feel about getting involved with a younger man? Would you be concerned about the opinion of your pastor or friends?" Chuck asked.

I was so nervous. I hesitated to answer. There was silence on the phone.

"Hello, Yevette, are you still there?"

"Yes, I'm here, I said.

"I don't know what to say," I said, blushing.

"Well I'd like for you to consider it," Chuck said.

"There's chemistry between the two of us, I have always been interested in you, and like to see where this will go," Chuck continued.

"Are you serious?" I asked.

My heart was beating as if it was going to come right out of my chest.

"Yes, I am," Chuck said, firmly.

"I'm going to have to really pray about this," I replied, seriously.

"Okay, well, you do what you have to do, and we will talk again soon alright?"

"Okay Chuck, goodnight," I said.

As time evolved, Chuck and I spoke often and became close. He called me in the morning, afternoon on his lunch breaks, and late in the evening to say goodnight. The attention I received from Chuck took my mind away from my problems, especially with Nichol.

The Devil is shrewd. He finally formed a weapon, to try and knock me out. The enemy was planting thoughts in my mind saying, 'You deserve to be happy, there's nothing wrong with having "a friend;" you can't spend all of your life worried about Nichol and everyone else.' I began to agree. The next thing I knew, I looked forward to the phone calls. I found myself waiting by the phone, made sure my phone was on, and was always available whenever Chuck called. He lived four hours away, so we only talked on the phone.

The feelings I had for Chuck grew stronger. My heart yearned for the attention. I had been swept off my feet, by a much younger man. I did not feel I was doing anything wrong. He was in another city, and we were only talking on the phone. 'What harm could that do?' I thought. I felt I had something to look forward to, even just for a moment.

Since Nichol had moved back home, I told her about Chuck and I reconnecting. She did not like the situation one bit. I was trying to find somewhere in the apartment to talk to Chuck in private one night. My nephew was there in our living room talking on his cell phone. Nichol was in the bedroom talking on her cell phone. I decided to go downstairs and get in my car to have some privacy.

After a couple of hours, Nichol came down to the car. She tapped on my window. I let the window down.

"What do you want," I said.

"Hey mom, I was upstairs minding my own business, and I heard the Lord say go tell your mother, out of the multitude of words, sin lacketh not," Nichol said.

I looked at her in disbelief. She stood at my car window with a serious expression on her face.

"You need to get out of this car and come upstairs, if you keep doing all this talking, you gonna end up talking about something ungodly," Nichol said.

I got convicted in my spirit. I knew it was God speaking through her.

"You're right, I'm coming up now," I said.

"Who is that?" Chuck asked.

"It's Nichol," I replied.

I relayed to him what Nichol said, told him goodnight, and went upstairs.

I was so grateful to God that he sent a warning to me. I made sure I was careful after that rebuke. The calls continued, and I felt like someone on drugs. I longed to hear his voice. This seducing spirit working through him was subtly drawing me away from my time with God.

Nichol came home early on a Saturday morning after being out at an afterhours club all night. She was sloppy drunk. I was up getting ready to go exercise. In her intoxicated state, she was talking about some guy she thought was cute.

"He's really cute mom," Nichol said, slurring.

"My friend Chuck is cute too," I said, jokingly.

Something rose up in Nichol as she began to cry.

"Mom, please! Don't you know the Devil wants you? He wants your anointing. The Devil can't come at you directly, he had to come in a roundabout way. That's why he sent Chuck. My very life depends on your prayers, and I can't afford for you to backslide Mom!" Nichol screamed, in tears.

The power of God engulfed the room where we were. I started to cry and speak in tongues. Nichol started to speak in tongues also. I took my blessed oil, poured it on her head, and entire body. We were so loud I woke up my nephew that was asleep in the next room. All of us began to pray and praise God. I laid hands on him also. When I left the house they both were prostrate on the floor under the anointing.

There was no more over-riding the Spirit of God. The Lord began to minister to me at the park. I realized that Chuck was sent on an assignment to distract. I did not want to forfeit the gifts that God had placed on my life. I cut all ties with Chuck. All kinds of distractions were coming at me to bring me false comfort.

God dispatched angels to intervene, and help as lust was after my anointing.

My Gay Ministry

Nichol took it to another level, I have never seen anything like it. We lived in the same house, but we were living two separate lifestyles. Her mindset was as if she had been incarcerated for seven years. She was so glad to be away from Candy.

Nichol bought another car, and started going out seven nights a week. It seemed like she began to smoke more cigarettes, marijuana, and use cocaine excessively. She was drinking alcohol like a fish. I was praying that she did not become an alcoholic. I never knew her to drink to this extent. It was getting ridiculous. She would smoke out in the hallway, but the fumes still came in under the door.

Nichol's friend was asleep on the couch one morning. I never known her to bring women home. Usually it was just her gay male friends.

"Hey who is that girl sleep on the couch," I asked, whispering.

"That's my best friend Cee Cee. You heard me talk about her Mom. You remember the transsexual I use to go visit?" she replied.

I was floored because I heard Nichol countless times talk about Cee Cee. I was in amazement that Cee Cee was born a man, but had no hint of masculinity. She looked better than most women. Wow! This transsexual was the most passable one I had seen. Any other time my discernment and "gaydar" (gay radar) would have tuned in.

My peace was greatly disturbed. I would get up in the morning and her friends were asleep all over the living room. It was a mess. Nichol started getting careless with the drugs. Sometimes she left them all over the house.

I would look out the window and watch her parking some mornings returning from all night excursions. She was so intoxicated, it was a miracle that she came home in one piece.

"Thank You Jesus!" is all I could say.

I undressed her and smeared anointing oil all over her body. "Devil let my baby go! I bind you up Satan in the name of Jesus," I said, praying over her inebriated being.

I started ministering to everyone that came home with her. Many of her friends were filled with Holy Ghost right in our living room. They would be stretched out on the floor speaking in tongues. I took them to church to be baptized in the name of JESUS.

I was a LIGHT in a DARK place.

The reality was I had a "gay" ministry. I ministered to Nichol's friends as I would anyone that I met on the street. These young people were broken, despondent, and lost. They all called me Mother.

I looked at Nichol's friends who were in that lifestyle as souls needing to be saved. I took the time to get to know them as a person. Many of her friends in the homosexual lifestyle shared with me about their upbringing. Most of them had been molested by family members.

Sometimes her friends came over and waited while Nichol was getting dressed. The Lord opened the door for me to minister to them. A few of them would change their minds and not want to leave our house with Nichol to go out clubbing. They felt the peace of God because I constantly was in prayer throughout that apartment.

One young guy, saw how I treated Nichol regardless of her appearance. I had made her dinner, and hot tea that night. He was visiting from out of town, and got turned out at an early age. He wanted some attention, and asked me if I could make him some hot tea, so I did. The young man got up on the sofa and told Nichol he did not want to go out.

"I'm staying here with mother," he said.

133

Another time I woke up in the middle of the night, as I often did. There was a young man sitting in the kitchen. Apparently he did not know I was in the bedroom. When I came to the kitchen, he seemed surprised to see me.

"Hello," I said to him.

"Hi," he said, surprised to see me.

Tears filled up in his eyes. I never met him before.

"Are you Esko's mom?" he asked.

(Nichol's street name was Esko).

"Yes, and what's your name?" I asked, with a welcoming voice.

"My name is David." he answered.

"I can't believe you're being so nice to me. It's the middle of the night and you're pleasant?"

"Awww", I said to him. "God woke me up just to talk to you," I replied.

"I never had anyone's parent be nice to me, because I'm gay they are usually so rude," David said.

He was so appreciative that I was kind to him. He began to share his heart. He came by often and visited me. He also called me Mother.

There was another young guy named Greg that was at Nichol's one night. He instantly bonded with me. He told me his whole life story. I never saw that young man before in my life, and never saw him again after that night.

Another young man named Ken occasionally came to visit. He felt so comfortable he curled up at the foot of my bed to watch TV. I called him my grandson. Nichol brought countless young men to meet "Mother" as they so affectionately called me.

Nichol's friend JB went to church with me one Sunday. Nichol had a hangover and did not go with us. He ended up getting baptized in Jesus name and filled with the Holy Ghost. I took pictures and videotaped it, so Nichol could see. She was surprised, but happy.

Nichol, had taken to the younger guys and called them her "nephews." They were much younger than her. I overheard her often, encouraging them not to waste their lives as she did partying. Though she was not in church, she did not stand in the way of me sharing the gospel with anyone.

I felt compassion for the gay community. It was so sad that most of them had no direction. Some were confused about their sexual identity. Many of them had been put out of their parent's house because of their choice to embrace the gay lifestyle.

I recall another young man coming by the house asking me to pray for him.

"What is it that you want prayer for?" I asked.

"For me and my boyfriend to have peace in our relationship." he answered.

"God can't give peace in a relationship that's against his order." I replied.

As a minister of the gospel, I had to give truth at all cost.

He seemed sad that God's approval was not on his sinful lifestyle. I tried to explain the scriptures to him that homosexuality was against the nature of God, but he seemed conflicted. The devil is such a deceiver. The Lord used me to display His love to lost souls.

"The devil is crazy, he tells the men they are women, and tells the women they are men," I said to Nichol one day. None of the people I met were truly happy in the gay lifestyle. Nobody knew each other's legal name. The lifestyle was such an illusion.

Nichol called at 6:00 AM one morning. I thought something was wrong. I braced myself.

"Mom hey wake up I got my three friends that need prayer," she said.

"Oh, okay Nichol I'm getting up now," I said.

They were walking through the door ten minutes later. They must have been close by. I grabbed my bottle of oil and greased up my hands. One by one I laid hands on them and bam! The power of God knocked them out.

Nichol and two of the guys were speaking in tongues. The other guy was crying out to God.

"Lord help! Why did this happen to me?" the young man said, kneeling. I found out afterward that he had been molested as a child by a family member.

I got on the floor with him and began to hug him as I ministered to him. I told him to start saying "Thank you Jesus!" Within moments he was speaking in tongues. His name was Jonathan, but they called him Whiz.

Nichol and Jonathan went to church that Sunday and he was baptized in the name of Jesus in Long Beach at an Apostolic church.

"How's your daughter doing?" Pastor Miley asked, right in front of Nichol.

He did not recognize her. I pointed at Nichol.

"There she is," I said.

He played it off well, but he was shocked.

"Oh, hi sweetheart," he said.

"Hi," Nichol said.

The Lord was still saving souls and even in the midst of my daughter's mess there was ministry.

The Lord constantly reminded me to show them love.

CeeCee

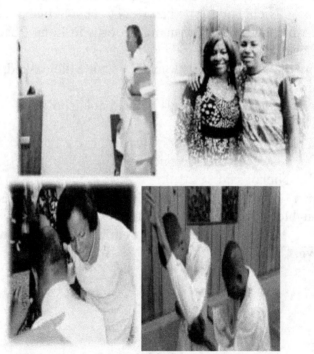

Nichol came to church for her friend (Whiz) Jonathan's Baptism

Death Traps

One Thanksgiving Eve, Nichol was going to stay with her friend named Cannon. Cannon was a "stud," which is an urban term for masculine lesbian. She sold drugs on a large scale. Nichol was on the phone with Cannon, and left the house in a celebratory mood. It was a few days before Nichol's birthday, so I guess they were going to hang out that night.

Later that night, I received a call from Nichol in a panic. She told me Cannon had been shot, and was in the hospital. I volunteered to pick Nichol up and take her. I did not want her to go alone.

We entered the hospital. There were all sorts of people in the waiting room. I could tell by their attire and demeanor that some were gang bangers, and others were lesbians. Cannon's girlfriend was there too. Nichol introduced me to Cannon's mother.
"This is my mom. She's a minister, and I would like for her to pray for Cannon if it's okay," Nichol said.
"Absolutely, I would be grateful for you to pray for daughter," she replied.

Immediately, her mom stopped anyone else from going back to visit Cannon. Nichol led me back to where her friend was. There was blood everywhere. The doctor had given her pain medicine, and she was able to talk in a low tone.

Some people tried to rob her for her drug money. Nichol was supposed to be with her, but was detoured by another phone call. God spared her life once again. God showed Nichol favor in the dark.

Soon as Cannon recovered, she got a glass eye. The bullet fragments pierced her eyeball, so they removed it in surgery. Nichol and her friend Cannon continued in their sin. They attended gay pride events in different states, partied at nightclubs, and dined at expensive restaurants.

Next stop, Las Vegas, Nevada. I was in Wal-Mart across the street from our house. Got a call from Nichol. She was hysterically, screaming in pain.

"Mom," she yelled.

"What's wrong?"

I detected in her voice there was something terribly wrong. She was breathing hard, gasping for breath.

"I can't breathe," she said.

She went on to tell me that she had been up for days partying, drinking, and using cocaine. She had cramps in her arms and her hand closed in a claw like position. Also, her shoulder hunched upward. She was scared.

"They're gonna let me die back here in the emergency room," she said.

I immediately went into prayer right there in Wal-Mart, calling on the name of Jesus!

Nichol had to get the name of the hospital from a nurse. She said they were making fun of her and looking at her in amazement that she was a woman. Finally, after dialing 911 to report their discrimination and negligence she received immediate care. She survived, and I was thankful.

Yet Nichol still was not ready to surrender. She wanted her space now that she was living even more of a party life. Almost daily she was coming home with new tennis shoes and clothes. She wanted me to get my own place because she was ready to get wild in her house. All our clothes combined were becoming cluttered, and even the two portable closets were full.

I began to pray and fast for direction in my life. After going on a three day fast, I received a call from my friend Kay in the Bay Area of Northern California.

"I felt led to call you," Kay said.

"Praise the Lord! I was sitting here waiting for an answer

from the Lord," I said, with a sigh of relief.

"I was supposed to call you earlier, but got distracted," Kay said.

Once I explained my dilemma to Kay she offered me to let me stay at her house for a month. This would give Nichol some space until I figured out where God was sending me. I already had a trip planned to go to Atlanta for my Niece Tanesha's college graduation. God instructed me to pack my boxes and he would lead me where to go. I packed twelve boxes, and they were in the middle of Nichol's living room.

Nichol was high every day. She was so out of control and moody; up one day down the next. You would think after that close call with death she would slow down. The Devil was stringing my baby along like a puppet.

If I had not stayed in God's presence I would have lost my mind.

Kay was visiting me in Los Angeles for a few days. I was just about to take her to the train station, and received a phone call from Nichol. She was downstairs in the back alley, sitting on the ground. Nichol had broken her ankle jumping down some woman's stairs. My friend and I picked her up off the ground. We put her in the car and took her to the hospital.

Her ankle was broken, which required emergency surgery. Since Nichol was high on cocaine they had to monitor her heart. She was caught in someone house. The girl busted Nichol laid up with her girlfriend and went to grab her Samurai sword off the mantle. The other guilty party tackled her own girlfriend to allow Nichol enough time to get dressed and run. Nichol fell down the steps on her untied shoestrings. She popped her right arm out of socket and fractured her ankle.

God was working behind the scenes. Nichol kept me on my knees. There were so many times God intervened on that child's behalf. He protected her through car accidents, robberies, shoot outs, and my main concern was that God would not allow her to go to jail.

The Lord always creates the opportunity to give him glory. While Nichol was getting x-rays in the emergency room, I went into the waiting area and began to pray for those that were waiting to be seen by the doctor. I was waiting for her to get surgery, and the Lord used me to minister to the nurse. I was in there laying hands on her and anointing her with blessed oil.

Nichol was in the hospital for about a week. They put a cast on her foot that came up her leg. Due to her shoulder being knocked out of socket she could not use the crutches to hold herself up. After she was home for a few weeks, Nichol figured a way to drive her car with the opposite foot. The devil drives you when you're under his influence. Nichol was partying with a cast on. She cut an opening in the screen window to throw the gate key down to guests that came to visit.

I went to Atlanta for my niece Tanesha's college graduation. Nichol insisted she would be fine getting around by herself. I thought I was going to stay in Atlanta and do ministry for a while. I did not have a peace about it, so after my short stay I returned to Los Angeles.

God started to deal with me about leaving my church of twenty-seven years. I prayed, and discussed it with my Pastor. It was hard to leave after being in that ministry so long, but I had to obey God. I know some people may have wondered why I did not leave fifteen years ago when my daughter was mistreated. The Lord had not released me to leave.

The power of God at that church kept me grounded. All the hell that I encountered as a result of Nichol's lifestyle was overwhelming. I sincerely loved my Pastor, and my church family. In spite of some of the things that transpired, there is no perfect church. God knew that the ministry had a leader of integrity. His dogmatic preaching kept me

141

examining myself.

I was led to go help a friend of mine at another church for about a year. After leaving that ministry, I established my own called Healing Waters Ministry. I began teaching seminars on how to effectively work the altar. I traveled to several locations in Northern California sharing the Gospel on my missionary journey.

Evang. Kay Chaney

Saga Continues

When I arrived home, Nichol informed me she was going to Atlanta. She was traveling with the same friend Cannon who lost her eye in a drug related robbery. Once she got to Atlanta she decided to stay past her vacation. I did not believe it was a good idea, but my opinion did not have much of an impact on her.

I prayed for God to close the door if it was not meant for Nichol to stay in Atlanta. I was always hopeful that God would miraculously straighten her life out. I learned it was best to take everything to the Lord in prayer. *The weapons of our warfare are not carnal, but mighty through God to the pulling down of strong holds* (2 Corinthians 10:4 KJV). **Sometimes when you give advice the flesh rebels against the truth, and does the opposite.**

Nichol was gone about three months. I woke up one morning with a bad feeling. My spirit was disturbed. I sensed something bad was going to happen. Immediately, my mind shifted to Nichol. I felt she was in some type of danger. I called her to see how things were going. There was some tension in her voice. The situation was not working out in Atlanta.

The next call I received, the friends she was staying with had been robbed. She was alarmed.

"Where are you?" I asked.

"I'm at Nya's house. She was going to invite a client over to pay for sex. I did not want to stay in the apartment while they engaged. I went outside and sat on the steps waiting until I heard him leave. When I went back into the house everyone in there was handcuffed with zip ties, and had been pistol-whipped (beaten with the gun) and robbed of their belongings," Nichol explained.

"Oh, my goodness are you serious?" I said.

"Guess what mom?" Nichol asked.

"What?" I answered.

"When I came in the house all my belongings were scattered in the middle of the floor, but nothing was taken. Mom I had no idea that you put white prayer cloths with blessed oil on them in my luggage. They were dumped on the floor," she said, surprisingly.

God brought back to my remembrance how one of the prayer warriors at my church told me to do that. Her name was Sister Marva and she had called one day before Nichol left for Atlanta. The power of God engulfed Sister Marva as she gave the instructions from the Lord.

Evang. Marva

"Listen here, God said get a white cloth and anoint it with oil, and cut it into pieces. Take the pieces of cloth and place them throughout everything Nichol owns," Marva said.

"Okay," I said.

"Now follow these instructions Vett. I believe God is going to honor it," Sister Marva said, confidently.

By faith, I did exactly what I was instructed to do.

At first, I thought maybe that's why my spirit was uneasy. The feeling never left even after I was relieved to know her life was spared. I called Nichol and warned her that she needed to come home. I told her I felt it was urgent that she leave Atlanta, and return to Los Angeles ASAP.

Nichol was aware how God used me, so she was convinced that my relationship with God was solid. She also knew I had a prayer life. When I stressed to her how serious it was to leave, she agreed to come home. One of my friends set up a buddy pass for her to leave within a day or two. I was unable to rest until her feet were back on California soil. Nichol came home on Saturday, October 27th.

149

The next morning, October 28th, I received a phone call from my older brother. He did not live far from us in Los Angeles. I saw his picture flash up on my cell phone caller ID.

"Praise the Lord," I answered.

"Praise the Lord," he said, with a cracking voice.

I knew that sound so well. My heart dropped as I awaited the news.

"What's wrong?" I asked, with hesitation.

After a long silence, he responded.

"It's Price. He's been murdered," he said.

"Oh no!" I screamed, "What happened?

"He was visiting a friend, and someone came in and killed both of them execution style," he said.

Saddened by the news, I took a moment to catch my breath. That call confirmed what I was feeling. Price was one of my younger brothers living in Atlanta. Nichol just returned from there. That was a dreadful day to receive such news.

My Beloved Brother Price

Everyone gathered at my oldest brother's house and made a pot of strong coffee. We began to network together to make funeral arrangements. We were no stranger to death. We already lost our father, mother, and two brothers. Not to mention several relatives over the years. There were eleven siblings total, and it seemed like they were leaving back to back.

Ironically, my brother Danny had just received a settlement. He purchased a ticket for me to go to Atlanta to officiate our brother's funeral. Nichol didn't even have the chance to unpack. I took her things out the suitcase and re-packed it with my stuff. I did not want to stay more than two or three days. The Lord instructed me to pack more clothes because I was going to be there for a while.

I preached my baby brother Price's funeral. God gave me strength during my grief. I ended up staying in Atlanta for two months. I ministered to countless people while in Atlanta. Five people were filled with the Holy Ghost during my stay.

While in Atlanta I reconnected with a woman name Jana. Jana and I met some years earlier in Los Angeles through a friend of mine. When I went back home after my brother's funeral, she and I stayed in touch. We connected spiritually, and spent time on the phone praying. She enjoyed talking about the things of God.

One afternoon Jana called and said things were shifting for her in Atlanta. She mentioned she might have to go back to the Midwest where she was from originally. Jana expressed to me that her mother was ill, and it didn't look good. She was reluctant to move back, though she was raised there, she had been away for over thirty years.

We began to fast and pray for direction in Jana's situation. Ultimately, she packed up and moved back to the place she resented. She called me one day to tell me she had been offered the opportunity to become the owner of an upscale Beauty Salon. I was so excited for her. She was keeping me up-to-date every day sending me pictures. She sent the picture when the new sign went up on the building. She showed me the various things that she was purchasing for the decor of the salon. Jana was blessed with a two-bedroom condo. Things were coming together for her. I was gladly rejoicing with her.

"I sure wish you could be here for my grand opening," Jana said, on the phone.

"Well, let me pray about it, I don't do anything without praying," I said.

Blind Faith

I absolutely had no idea or plans to living in a different state, let alone the Midwest where it snows. I had never been there even for a visit. I did not know anyone that lived in that region of the United States. I had been waiting for an answer, wondering where was I was going to end up for ministry. God shut the door to every avenue in Los Angeles, and I couldn't get an apartment. After the Lord instructed me to leave my church of twenty-seven years, I was solely dependent on God.

I had twelve boxes taped up in Nichol's living room. I knew I was going somewhere. I just did not know the destination. I went to a church meeting one evening in a nearby city. I had never been to this particular church before. There were just a few people in the service that night. This was a well-known prophet, who had been on the radio for many years. As the prophet was preaching he looked at me, and came off the pulpit.

"Your ministry is no longer here in Los Angeles, it's in a whole other state," he said.

He was waving his hand as if he was gesturing to a faraway location. I was sitting there in amazement waiting for more instructions. I was anticipating on him saying what city or state that it was. He never said where.

God gave me a peace about going to Jana's grand opening. I also received two more confirmations that I was released to go. I was not sure how long I was going to be gone, or where I was going when I left. I asked Jana if I could I bring my boxes with me. She was so excited that I was going to be able to attend her event.

"I have two bedrooms and two baths. You will have your own room and bathroom while you're here," she said.

This would be the first time that I ever lived outside of California, and that far away from Nichol. God had a plan that I knew not of. I was glad for the change. I had been fasting, and praying and seeking for God's direction. Now it seemed I was on my way to my destiny.

I just wanted some peace. There was nothing else that I could do to convince Nichol to return to what she knew was right. It seemed she was so far out there. The harder I prayed the worse she got. I knew the only one that could reach her was God. If he did not do it, it would not get done.

I exhausted all resources. There was a team of prayer warriors that prayed for her constantly. So many people loved Nichol. We remained hopeful she would get restored, and succeed in life. Many times, I released this burden to the Lord; then many times I would pick it back up again. It was hard to see such a brilliant young woman throw her life away in gangs, drugs, and debauchery (excessive indulgence in sensual pleasures).

As I was preparing to leave the Lord told me to 'Make haste! Someone is waiting on you.' I arrived a few days before the 4th of July. Jana introduced me to two women that she had grown up with. The next day I went to the salon with Jana so that she could show me around. The place was gorgeous. I was in a new world. The condo was beautiful, I had my own bedroom and bathroom. Her place with fashionably decorated.

God made it clear to me why he told me to make haste. There was a young girl that Jana hired that needed to be saved. I conversed with her the first day that I met her. The next day God allowed me to pray with her to receive the gift of the Holy Ghost. She was in the break room speaking in tongues. She quit shortly afterward to return to whatever state she was from. She and her boyfriend had split up.

The Grand Opening

The grand opening was finally here. I was so excited for a change. I was embracing my new city. Jana did everything first class. I began to help Jana at the salon. She had a public relations person to handle all her business. A TV station covered the opening, as well as a radio station. It was a very nice grand opening.

She did not mind that I prayed with people in the salon. Her friends began to receive the Holy Ghost. I prayed with her employees and some of them received the Holy Ghost. The nail technician and I clicked soon as we met. Her name was Vonna, and she received the Holy Ghost in the salon. I took her to an Apostolic Church to be baptized in the name of Jesus.

It was like a rushing mighty wind came through that salon. I was laying hands on people. Some received their healing, while many others got prayer and were encouraged. Jana appointed me as the salon coordinator. The power of God rested in that establishment.

Two young ladies came in one day to fill out an application for employment. They somehow noticed I had just come out the office praying. As one of them was leaving, she asked me if I could pray for her. She broke out and started speaking in tongues and laid out at the entrance of the salon.

Later another woman came in to get a job. She was a was a member of an Apostolic Church where she had been the church secretary for twenty years. After Jana hired her, I asked if I could go to church with her one day. Ironically, the Pastor was initially from Los Angeles and had been a member of the late Bishop Robert W. Mc Murray's church.

I was allowed full access to use their baptismal pool

whenever I needed to baptize someone with whom I had shared the plan of salvation. One day the secretary took me to the church and the Lord allowed me to baptize four women. We had a wonderful time in the Lord that day. They all went down in the name of the Lord Jesus!

Jana hired a young guy for a nail technician position. We found out later that his license was only valid in another state. His dad came in one day to get a manicure and we were introduced.

"What kind of car do you drive?" his dad asked.

"I just moved here from Los Angeles and I gave my car away before I left," I said.

"My name is Mr. Coburn. If you ever decide you want a car here's my card. Come and see me when you're ready," he replied.

"Thank you," I said.

I had no plans to permanently stay in the Midwest. However, as time went by, it was apparent that I was going to need a car. I was trusting in God. I did not know where I was going. I was leaning to my own understanding thinking I was going to end up down south in Atlanta, Georgia.

I was relying on Jana for transportation. I was taking a walk one morning, and praying about a car. The Lord let me know he had already sent the person to me to get a car. I called the car salesman. God is so good to me; the salesman drove over to the salon to pick me up and take me to the car dealership. He already had a car picked out for me.

The Lord told me whatever car he gives you take it. He suggested a beautiful 2010 Ford Fusion. The car had a sunroof top, and was equipped with everything I needed to drive in the snow. I did not put any money down. He told me a deposit was needed toward my car insurance. I did not have any money.

"I will pay your down payment for you. You're a woman of God and you need a car because the snow is coming," Mr. Coburn said.

"Really, I appreciate that. Thank you, Jesus!" I said.

I was ecstatic to have my own car again. The salesman programmed Gospel music on my radio, and I drove back to the salon rejoicing.

His son never returned to the salon. Ultimately, he was only there for me to make a connection with his dad.

What a mighty God we serve!

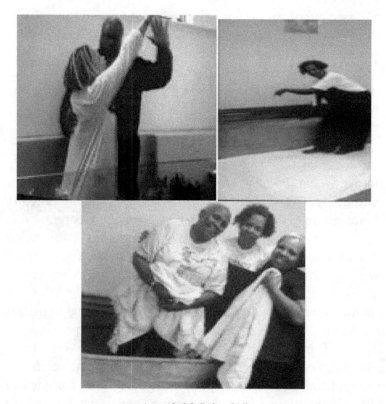

Acts 2:38 John 3:5
I baptized 5 women in Jesus name
Here is water what hinders you from being baptized? Acts 8:36

Set-up for a Blessing

Jana began displaying some ungodly actions. Her character changed. She started dating an unsaved man. He was coming over frequently. Jana and her boyfriend were going to clubs and drinking. I knew my stay at Jana's was coming to a close.

Can two walk together except they be agreed.
Amos 3:3 (KJV)

Nichol called early one morning. It was 6:30 am in California. Again, I thought something must have been wrong. 'What could be wrong now,' I thought as I braced myself.

"Mom, hey where's Jana I need to speak with her," Nichol said.

"Girl, what? Jana? What do you need to talk to her about? I asked, baffled.

"I must tell her what the Lord said. Get her on the phone," she said.

"She is gone to the beauty supply. You sound like you are intoxicated. Is this a joke?" I said.

"Call her on 3 way this is important," she said.

I made a conference call to Jana.

"Hey Jana, my daughter Nichol wants to talk to you. She is on 3-way," I said.

"Hello good morning Jana. The Lord has given me a message for you, so I want to get this off me. It's on me very strong. I never met ya and don't know ya. The Devil is going to try and come between you and my mom. If you don't leave that man alone you're going to lose everything you have," Nichol said.

Jana paused, and then tried to drown Nichol out with a boisterous prayer in a preaching tone. It was all an act that

158

Jana was doing. I did not discern God anywhere in Jana's prayer.

The ladies that I baptized asked me if I was going to stay and get my own place.

"My own place, here?" I asked.

I could not imagine staying in a city that I did not have any family or friends. One of the ladies called to give me a list of apartments. There were three apartments on the list. She insisted I go see a particular building first.

"Go see the first one on the list. It's a brand-new building Vett, it just opened," she said.

"Okay sounds great!" I said.

It was nobody but God. My steps were ordered by the Lord. The building was absolutely beautiful with all sorts of amenities. My new residence was just built from the ground up, and had only been open for two months. There was only one apartment left. I filled out the application and completed the necessary requirements. I was in love with the building. I never went to look at the other buildings that were on my list.

I was in prayer as I waited for an answer from the management company. My friend, prophet Mac, called.

"Woman of God! Keep your boxes packed. God said you will be moving within two days," he said.

"Thank you, Jesus! I cried.

"I see you running through your new apartment praising God and speaking in tongues," he said.

Later that evening I attended a church service. The speaker began to prophesy.

"Somebody in here is waiting on some papers to be released. I see them sitting on a desk. God's going to release those papers," the preacher said.

I began to rejoice. One of the requirements for me to move into my apartment was to have a doctor fill out a medical form.

159

The next day I went to the doctor's office to check the status of my paper work. The receptionist returned with an apology.

"I am so sorry; the paper was already signed. It was sitting on the doctor's desk, and it should have been faxed to the apartment office days ago," she said.

I asked them to give me the paper, so I could return it to the apartment office, since it was one block away.

"Tell them to give you your keys," the Holy Spirit spoke in my ear.

I did not hesitate to obey. I walked in the office.

"Here's the paper you were waiting on. You all need to give me my keys," I said, smiling.

"We were waiting to contact your daughter for a reference, but haven't been able reach her," the manager said.

The two women that worked in the office glanced at one another smiling.

"Give her the keys," the manager said to them.

She reached in the file cabinet drawer, and gave me the keys to my new place. My name was already on the white key pass. I thanked them as I took the keys. The Lord gave me favor.

"Go ahead and move in, we can fill the paperwork out later," the manager said.

I cried as I drove back to Jana's to pack my things into my car. I moved in with no money down. It was a two months later when the management company had me to complete the rest of my paperwork.

Labor Day weekend 2013, I moved into my brand new apartment. I was the first tenant to ever live in the unit. All I had when I moved in was twelve boxes of clothes. There was a brand-new refrigerator, stove, dishwasher, and a microwave.

Every floor had a laundry room. There was flat screen TV's on every floor in the hallway. On the first floor was a large community room with a 55-inch TV and fireplace. Down the hall on the same floor was a smaller room called the TV lounge, fully furnished. The second floor there was an activity room fully furnished, with a pool table, and TV. On the third floor there was an exercise room, also a TV. Lastly, on the fourth floor, which was my floor was a beautiful library, and computer lab combined. This new building was certainly the answer to my prayer. God had shown me favor. The prophecy had come to past, I moved exactly within two days.

I called to tell Nichol the great news.

"I have two bedrooms, one extra for you," I said.

"That is amazing, and God moved really fast. I'm not moving out of California mom," she said, laughing.

Nichol had purchased an iPhone. She called me to video chat as she was inside of the cell phone store. We had not seen each other in a year. She cried as she looked at me on camera. I gave her a tour of my new apartment, and she was so happy for me. I showed her the room that I previously mentioned to her.

"Why do you keep telling me there's an extra room?" Nichol said.

"Well I want you to know you are welcome here," I said.

"I'm not moving from California!" she said, in an adamant tone.

Just as my daughter had prophesied a word of warning, Jana was evicted from that condo. The salon shut down a year after it was opened. That unsaved man bought her down financially and spiritually. I was surprised how God used Nichol in an intoxicated state, but then again, in the Bible it records he spoke through a donkey.

Hammer Time

I was excited for what God was doing for me. The Lord was guiding me every step of the way. Nichol was always on my heart and in my prayers. The only peace I had was when I was working for the Lord. I had to keep it moving. Twenty years had passed interceding for Nichol. If it had not been for the almighty God, I would have given up.

Through it all, I trusted God's word and promises.

Nichol called me one day as I sat in my new apartment. She was upset. Her friend Jonathan that I took to get baptized owed her money. I could tell that she had been drinking or getting high.

"I'm going over there to get my money," she said.

I tried to talk her out of going to confront him. Her judgment was totally off. She would not listen to me. I was two-thousand miles away from Los Angeles. I got a little nervous as I tried to reason with her.

"You don't need to go Nichol," I begged.

"Nah, I can't let this slide," she said, angrily.

Nichol did not want to hear what I had to say. She hung up the phone. I got on my knees and began to pray. The next phone call I received from her she was devastated.

"What's going on?" I said, nervously.

"They jumped me mom," she said, frantically.

"Who?" I responded.

She went on to tell the story. Nichol had gone to the person's house. The guy that owed her the money had a friend flicking a switchblade. She said since the guy had a knife she pulled out a hammer from her pants. As Nichol and Jonathan argued; the other guy crept up from behind, snatched the hammer, and clobbered her in the head with it.

163

She was knocked off the sidewalk into the street. The man straddled over her as she held up her arms to block the blows. Someone videotaped the whole incident, and blasted it all over Facebook.

My heart dropped as I listened. I felt so helpless. Suddenly, I heard the voice of the Lord.

"I had to take her this way. Calm down, it's all right I'm in control," the Holy Spirit said.

Immediately, a peace came over me.

There is a peace that only comes from God, that surpasses all understanding.

"Are you injured? Do you need to go the hospital?" I said, nervously.

"No," she cried.

Nichol was in shock. It was a sobering moment for her.

We sat silent for a while.

"What are you going to do now?" I asked.

"I'm going to Uncle Wendell's house," she said.

Nichol went directly to my brother Wendell's house. He lived about six blocks from her. Her Aunt Dee put an ice pack on a small lump on top of her head. Nichol was beat with a hammer, and miraculously suffered no injury. Her aunt kept her woke for a while to make sure she did not have a concussion.

"God literally knocked some sense into me Mom," she said.

At that very moment God turned it around! The Holy Ghost arrested her. The next day, without hesitation, Nichol went to our home church with her uncle and aunt. Since I knew she was going I watched the service on live stream. It was a week before Christmas.

As I watched the service, suddenly during the altar call the whole spirit shifted. I saw people crying, shouting, and running across the church. At first, I could not see Nichol, but then the camera zoomed in on her. Nichol stood there with a bald fade and dressed in men's clothing, with tears streaming down her face.

That same woman Sister Marva, who had instructed me to anoint the white cloths, was praying for Nichol. My other good friend, who Nichol called Auntie Lona, got right in her ear and was ministering to her. I saw her hands up in the air surrendering to God. The next thing I knew the power of God knocked her back on the floor. She was crying uncontrollably.

I was way across country watching on my TV screen. The mighty hand of God was destroying the yokes of bondage off my baby. Nichol finally was tired of sin. There was nowhere else for her to run. God said that is enough, it is over.

I received calls from relatives and friends excited about Nichol being at church. They had taken pictures of Nichol slain in the spirit in front of the altar. My nephew took pictures of Nichol getting prayer. Whew! Twenty years! God let her know that the heavens do rule. Now her true deliverance could begin.

God is absolute. When He shuts something down, he makes sure it is clear. All of Nichol's friends turned their back on her for various reasons. She no longer sold drugs. Somehow a lie was circulating that she was an informant for the police. Her life was in jeopardy. Nichol had wrecked her car twice, and had a lawsuit pending.

Nichol fell out with the "gay sorority" she was involved with for twenty years. She was exposed to so much while being out there. It is unbelievable the way my little church girl's life turned out. It was all in God's plan. It was her designated time as a sheep that had gone astray to return unto the Shepherd and Bishop of her soul (1 Peter 2:25).

I BELIEVED GOD! I KNEW HE DID NOT BRING HER THIS FAR TO LET HER DIE IN THE STREETS.

The Brutal Hammer Attack Miraculously No Injury

The next day she was crying out at the altar

December 14,2014 God began to change my Daughter's Life!

The Manifestation

Eventually, Nichol began living her life as a hermit. She was scared to leave the house for fear that someone would harm her. We spoke on the phone often, since her friends turned against her. That was God allowing them to part ways. After fifteen years in her apartment selling drugs, she wanted to move to a new location.

Nichol started to join me on a prayer line every night. She gave a prayer request to the prophet.

"I would like to receive prayer for direction, I need to move," she said.

"I believe if you go east, you'll find a place to live," the prophet said.

"Thank you," Nichol said.

Immediately I thought moving here with me was east. I use to show her my extra room on face time, and tell her I had enough space for her. She did not want to leave Los Angeles. Initially, I did not want to leave either, but God set me up for a blessing because of my obedience.

After weeks of looking for an apartment in neighboring cities east of Los Angeles, she realized she needed a fresh start. My good friend from Georgia named Prophet Mac called.

"Hey, Evangelist can you contact your daughter? I got a word for her," he said.

"Yes, hold on let me try to get her on the line," I replied.

I called Nichol on a three-way.

"Hello, honey, my friend Prophet Mac wants to give you a word from the Lord." I said.

"Oh, okay," Nichol said, hesitantly.

"Woman of God," he said.

It was silence. Nichol did not respond.

"Woman of God," he repeated.

"Yes sir," Nichol replied.

"Make haste! There is a hit out on your life," he said.

"Wow!" I said.

"I see you in a vision packing a suitcase. As long as you obey God you will remain under his divine protection," he said.

"Yes sir, I knew the Devil was trying to assassinate me," Nichol said.

That confirmed to me that some of her friends of over ten years were snakes. They had been calling me to confide that my daughter had begun using methamphetamine and was behaving bizarre. It was clear they were plotting her assassination, by trying to make it appear as if, "she was so out of control God only knows what will happen." Nichol kept emphasizing being on the road to sobriety. She was campaigning on social media "21 days to break a habit." Furthermore, she was not on meth, but her addiction was to cocaine. The Lord resolved any suspicions that I had, so I blocked their numbers.

The last friend left out the bunch was a stud named Chili, but I called her by her real name Shonda. They were friends for the entire time Nichol had been in that lifestyle. One night Shonda was over Nichol's house when I called. I knew she had been going to church with Nichol as of lately.

"Hi Miss Rivers," Shonda said, in the background.

Nichol put the phone on speaker.

"Hi sweetie! How are you?" I replied.

"I'm fine. Can I ask you a question about the bible?" Shonda asked.

"Sure, you can," I answered.

I don't remember what she asked, but I did have some dialogue about the word of God concerning her inquiry.

"Shonda do you want to be filled with the Holy Ghost?" I asked.

"I sure do Miss Rivers," she said.

"Nichol get the oil and anoint her head," I said.

"Okay Mom," Nichol replied.

"Shonda, I want you to open your mouth and praise God by saying, Thank you Jesus! because the Holy Ghost is a gift, so thank Him in advance," I said.

Within about fifteen minutes Shonda was speaking in tongues.

The Devil was still on Nichol's trail trying to lure her back into the world. She almost went to Las Vegas for one last Gay Pride; but God shut that down when He revealed it to Prophet Mac. Former associates were popping by yelling her name from downstairs, enemies were firing gun shots outside, and she overheard a plot against her as she was accidentally pocket-dialed. I suggested going to stay with her uncle for a while to let the turmoil at that apartment phase out.

Nichol kept going to church on a regular basis. She decided to join City of Refuge Under the leadership of Bishop Noel Jones following another offense which occurred at our home church. My friend Dr. Willis was an instructor at the New Members class. She volunteered to give Nichol some women's clothes that following Sunday. I was overjoyed to hear the excitement in my baby's voice. She had a look of relief in her countenance I could clearly discern when we video-chatted.

Another friend of mine that was a prophet named Shannon also blessed Nichol with some money. Nichol was so thankful. She went to buy a wig, and some 2-inch pumps she called "Lil Debbie's." The Korean salesman at the beauty supply, generally known for aggressive upselling laughed hysterically at the wigs she tried on. I knew the Devil was trying to discourage this transition back to her natural state. It was Mother's Day weekend 2015 that my baby dressed as a woman after almost twenty years. She looked gorgeous when she called me on the camera.

Nichol was not trying to leave Los Angeles. She thought by moving to the suburbs she would be fine. We would look for apartments online over the phone together all day. I figured God would lead her to me or elsewhere. I stayed prayerful.

Nichol said she was watching TBN and Bishop Jakes was on. At that split second that she turned up the volume he was yelling.

"Make haste, make haste, make haste, make haste!" Bishop Jakes commanded through the TV screen.

Nichol said her body was covered in goose bumps as she felt God's presence in her room. That confirmed to Nichol that she needed to move out of the state of California. She embraced the change, and told me she was moving here with me. I was elated.

God began to move miraculously on Nichol's behalf. He really wanted her to know that He was with her. Shonda told her where she could sell her clothes, and her tennis shoes. Nichol was mentally overwhelmed as she bagged up all her belongings. She was calling me every step of the way. The stores paid her a nice sum of money.

Her cousin Pooh received an unexpected check in her account. It allowed her to purchase Nichol's car. The day before she left Los Angeles, the lawyer's office called and said they had a check for her. Nichol had over $5,000 to jump start her women's wardrobe. She wanted me to take her shopping once she got here.

Nichol left a furnished apartment behind. The ticket that the Lord told her to book was $400 one way. She could not make sense of that. Nichol was hoping to stay in California until after the 4th of July for a family cookout. Our relatives were flying in to celebrate the holiday. Nichol obeyed God and booked that costly flight with two layovers. She could not figure out why God insisted taking this flight.

June 15, 2015 Nichol was embarking upon a new journey. She boarded that flight out of Los Angeles with great anticipation. God divinely orchestrated her steps. A woman boarded the same plane on her first layover and prophesied during the flight. Nichol called me while waiting for the connecting flight.

"Mom this lady was next to me on the plane. She said God will avenge me with the people that set me up and I would hear about it. She also said the peace I am pursuing would be found when my feet touch new soil," Nichol said.

"Really that's something. Oh my goodness," I said.

"Yes, I can't believe God revealed all that to her," she said.

"God's ways are past finding out. Jesus loves you baby," I replied.

If Nichol would have leaned to her own understanding and taken a different flight, she would have missed that divine connection.

God's divine timing crossed their paths.

We had a great time bonding after years of going in two separate directions. Since she had been living as man for twenty years, we had to buy everything including undergarments. Our summer was very adventurous while literally reconstructing her image. We visited several churches in the city, went to the movies, ate at restaurants, and walked at parks. It reminded me of when she was younger.

Nichol began going through a series of deliverance. She was so hungry for God. She spent hours locked in her room speaking in tongues. Nichol completed some renunciations, which breaks legal agreement with the works of darkness. She fasted for three days a week for seven months. That girl was serious about not having any residue. All the learned behavior of street slang, masculine gestures, and hoodlum attitude had to be broken. The more cognizant she became of acting feminine the easier it was to naturally embrace it.

After getting some counseling, I could see Nichol socially evolving. She was so used to being in the same environment for years. She was paranoid at first making this adjustment. God was truly working a miraculous transformation right in front of me. Nichol wanted to be re-baptized in the name of Jesus for her "conscience sake" (1 Peter 3:21). She evolved from a caterpillar to a butterfly.

Nichol started doing a broadcast on Periscope titled "Burning the Midnight Oil." She was teaching bible study nightly. The Lord instructed her to share her testimony. She was not sure how people would respond. Nichol turned on TBN Network again, and Bishop Jakes was on the screen.
"He who the Son sets FREE is FREE indeed!" Bishop TD Jakes said, while preaching.

Nichol jumped up and ran through the house speaking in tongues and praising God. She said the weight of condemnation lifted off her shoulders. She was joyful. I could feel the shift into the dawning of a new day.
"*There is therefore now no condemnation to them which are in Christ Jesus who walk not after the flesh, but after the Spirit.*" Romans 8:1 (KJV)

From that day forward, she has been unashamedly sharing her testimony. Her book was completed a year after she got here. "Behind Enemy Lines" is her riveting autobiography. Nichol has been a guest on several radio stations, and a few Christian television broadcasts. She has been reaching the masses with her story of deliverance.

All those years that Nichol was bound, the enemy thought he won! The Devil fought her so hard, because he knew the anointing that was on her life. He tried to kill her, but God said, "Not so! She shall live and not die and declare the works of the Lord!" No demon in Hell could stop what God had prepared for Nichol! Now I'm rejoicing for all that I went through. God kept me in the midst of it all.

We must trust God as we go through our wilderness experience. Faith is not knowing what the end will be. I held on to God's word and did not deny His name. I had to set my emotions to the side and focus on a victorious outcome. It was difficult to remain positive after years had gone by. A mother's love and passion for God caused me to keep believing.

"We walk by faith, and not by sight." 2 Corinthians 5:7

It is important to pay attention to different signs. I know in my case, I had so much transpiring in my personal life that I missed a few clues. Keeping the lines of communication open is the best way to stay abreast to your child's development. As parents we cannot be so intimidating, that we put such a fear in our children, which inhibits them from disclosing personal issues.

Society has become desensitized to same sex relationships. Satan has promoted a platform for 'perversion' as if it is normal behavior. The root of homosexuality is rejection, which becomes intertwined with deception. The laws have been passed legalizing these unions, and I am not surprised at this occurring since the stage for the Anti-Christ is being set.

"Neither shall he regard the God of his fathers, nor the desire of women, nor regard any god; for he shall magnify himself above all (Daniel 11:37 KJV).

Homosexuality is a manifestation of something deeper.

Many have been sexually abused, have low self-esteem, and suffer from rejection. Statistics prove the "gay genes" theory to be false. The Holy Bible is our moral compass. In the book of Genesis, God commanded in the Garden of Eden to be fruitful and multiply. You cannot pro-create with the same sex.

This spirit attacks children when they are impressionable and vulnerable. The spirit of homosexuality is "unnatural lust." God can deliver anyone from this stronghold. If you want to be set free you must be determined.

Making sure that you search the scriptures for yourself is important (John 5:39). Jesus gave a mandate in the word of God that must be followed as a requirement to enter into the Kingdom.

*Jesus answered, "Very truly I tell you, no one can enter the kingdom of God unless they are born of water and the Spirit." * John 3:5 (NIV)

The only way to constitute the New Birth is to put your faith and belief in action. Contained in Acts 2:38 is the New Testament plan of Salvation. Our resurrected Savior wants to impart that same Spirit that raised Him up from the grave in you. Acts 2:4, Acts 8:14-17, Acts 10:44-48, and Acts 19:1-6 are all consistent biblical signs that speaking in tongues is the evidence that you have received the Holy Spirit. This spiritual battle cannot be conquered without being empowered (Acts 1:8).

The churches must globally embrace the blueprint in the book of Acts to see an impact in their region. Leaders must teach as it relates to scripture. You cannot change the word of God in order to support what you believe. You have to take the word of God for what it literally says. There is no way to change the word because it is infallible without error.

*"Then Peter said unto them, Repent and be baptized every one of you in the name of Jesus Christ for the remission of sins, and ye shall receive the gift of the Holy Ghost. For the promise is unto you, and to your children, and to all that are afar off, even as many as the Lord our God shall call. * Acts 2:38-39 (KJV)

I pray that all those who read this book have been encouraged. You are victorious in any test you may encounter. God is a mighty deliver! *He can do exceedingly, abundantly, more than we can ask or think* (Ephesians 3:20b KJV). He will never put more on us than we can bear. I understand that when you are facing adversity all those scriptures seem irrelevant. Do not stop interceding for your child.

If the Lord did it for my daughter, rest assured that He is no respecter of persons.

My only regret is that I didn't always have peace during my trials. There were moments I allowed situations to get the best of me. In spite of opposition, I realized that my praise kept my sanity. Responding in my own intellect at times pushed my daughter further away. If I could rewind the time, I wouldn't have interfered with God's process. I was not called to be a Savior to a soul that was loaned to me, and that God had shed his blood for.

The enemy wants us to give up on our loved ones, but we must speak life over every situation. It does not matter what it appears to look like on the outside; *"Pray without ceasing"* (1 Thessalonians 5:17). <u>God does not want us to be driven by emotions.</u> As parents we must learn to love the way God does, which is full of compassion. Be careful not to allow sentimental and emotional ties to get in the way. Emotions are tied to our senses, and can delay the process. God has our plans in the palm of his hand.

It is said, "It takes a village to raise a child." I believe that it takes the power of the Holy Ghost to deliver a prophet of God from the snares of the devil. It was the prayers of the righteous, and a determined Mother that refused to see her child die in sin.

That Devil had no choice, but to let my baby go!

God's "Mission was accomplished."

CATERPILLAR 2 BUTTERFLY

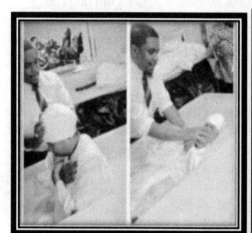

RIP My Sis Yvonne 8-4-16

MINISTRY MOGULS

Pastor LeAundre & Casey Bumpus

Dorinda ClarkCole

Lady Karen Clark-Sheard

Evangelist Sandra Riley

Kierra Sheard

Dr. Dorinda Clark-Cole

Bishop Eric & Shenita Lloyd

Bishop George "Awesome" Dawson

GEI C.O.G.I.C. Dr. Dorinda Cole   Dr.- Bishop Jackie McCullough

Dr.-Bishop Pat McKinstry   Dr. Dorinda Clark-Cole

Dr.-Bishop Iona Locke   Prophet Carn

TCT Network Bishop Larry Mack

189